MULTINATIONAL COMPUTER SYSTEMS

MULTINATIONAL
COMPUTER
SYSTEMS

An Introduction
To Transnational Data Flow
And Data Regulation

Harry Katzan, Jr.

Chairman, Computer Science Department
Pratt Institute

International Series on
Data Communications and Networks

VNR **VAN NOSTRAND REINHOLD COMPANY**
NEW YORK   CINCINNATI   ATLANTA   DALLAS   SAN FRANCISCO
LONDON   TORONTO   MELBOURNE

Van Nostrand Reinhold Company Regional Offices:
New York   Cincinnati   Atlanta   Dallas   San Francisco

Van Nostrand Reinhold Company International Offices:
London   Toronto   Melbourne

Copyright © 1980 by Litton Educational Publishing, Inc.

Library of Congress Catalog Card Number: 80–10720
ISBN: 0-442-21573-8

Manufactured in the United States of America

Published by Van Nostrand Reinhold Company
135 West 50th Street, New York, N.Y. 10020

Published simultaneously in Canada by Van Nostrand Reinhold Ltd.
15   14   13   12   11   10   9   8   7   6   5   4   3   2   1

Library of Congress Cataloging in Publication Data

Katzan, Harry.
  Multinational computer systems.
  (International series on data communications and networks)
  Includes bibliographical references and index.
  1.   International business enterprises—Management—Data processing.   2.   Management
information systems.
I.   Title.
HD69.17K33   658′.049′02854   80–10720
ISBN 0-442-21573-8

International Series on
Data Communications and Networks

Multinational Computer Systems: An Introduction to Transnational Data
  Flow and Data Regulation, Harry Katzan, Jr.

FOREWORD

Silently and relentlessly, the technology of computers and telecommunications has been expanding, amoeba-like, moving this way and that, engulfing the information systems of society. From the relatively simple credit records of the local department store to the most complex information systems spanning continents by way of satellite, electronic technology is transforming our way of life.

Along with its advantages, the electronic information society has also brought unanticipated complications and even danger to our personal privacy, to the character and texture of our national life, and to relationships with our friends and foes around the world. These dangers stem not from any conspiracy to deprive individuals or even nations of their privacy and autonomy. Rather, because the technology of collecting, storing, retrieving, and disseminating information has developed so explosively, there has not been time for the gradual evolution of the social mores, laws, and treaties needed to deal with it.

Thus, the problem takes on major international proportions, affecting relations between those nations having pre-eminence in computer and telecommunications technology, and those lagging behind—both developed nations and developing nations. Canada, for instance, is concerned that the southward flow of data for servicing in the United States—because of our technical superiority—is causing a drain on its economy. Brazil is alarmed that permitting data to move in and out for processing purposes will force a dependence on foreign corporations, constituting a new form of colonialism—this time through telecommunications networks.

It has been difficult to understand the scope of this dynamic problem due to the lack of adequate literature setting forth the broad and complex ramifications of the issues. This timely work by Professor Harry Katzan, Jr., helps fill that need.

DAVID F. LINOWES

PREFACE

Among the major problems facing multinational organizations are controlling and monitoring the growth of computer facilities across national boundaries. Multinational computer systems are relatively easy to justify because of the economic factors involved, and computer decisions are frequently made without due regard to the problems inherent in the technology and in the organizational and international environment. The primary objective of *Multinational Computer Systems* is to translate the technical, political, and economic issues of multinational computer systems into a coherent and readable form accessible by executives, managers, and decisionmakers. While the issues are relevant to computer decisions, the subject matter itself should be of interest to all persons involved with international business. The contents of the book are covered in six chapters and seven appendixes. The chapters cover the following topics:

- Overview of data regulation
- Notes on liberty, freedom, and rights
- Information technology
- Personal privacy in recordkeeping systems
- Approaches and activities in data regulation and transborder data flow
- Multinational systems

The appendixes give resource documents on various aspects of the subject matter.

Multinational Computer Systems is concerned with personal privacy in recordkeeping systems and with transnational data flow as they relate to four general classes of multinational systems:

- International computer-service companies
- On-line systems of multinational organizations

- International service networks
- Distributed systems

These systems have a wide international impact, and several governments believe the regulation of transborder data flow to be a new challenge and a new obligation. Thus, this book covers the subjects of transnational data flow and data regulation from several points of view and represents technical, economic, and political factors.

The book is intended for executives, managers, and decisionmakers concerned with multinational computer systems and transborder data flow. The reader need not have a computer background to benefit from it.

It is a pleasure to acknowledge the insight and cooperation of Larry Hager, senior editor, Van Nostrand Reinhold Company, who had the foresight to publish a book on the groundbreaking subject of multinational computer systems; the contribution of Alberta Gordon in expertly managing the complex task of producing the book; and the editing of Patricia Mansfield, who greatly improved the quality of the book. My wife Margaret assisted with manuscript preparation and was an excellent partner during the entire project.

HARRY KATZAN, JR.

CONTENTS

1
OVERVIEW OF DATA REGULATION

It is a paradox, but perhaps we have to regulate the free flow in order to keep it free.

JAN FREESE*

To the layman, the widespread use of computer-based information systems must seem like a revolution, equivalent, at least in scope and magnitude, to the invention of movable type for book printing. The printed word has enabled the average person to become literate and thereby to actively participate in the dynamics of modern society. The rapid expansion of information technology, however, has made a lot of people illiterate on the subject of computers. Their natural reaction, in many instances, has been to believe that computers and computer people exist in a world of their own.

Expansion of information technology

To persons in the computer field, the task of staying abreast of a rapidly expanding technology has left little time and energy with which to be concerned with the social impact of the marriage of computer science and telecommunications. Because early data processing systems were simply mechanized versions of easily understood manual methods, the evolution of information technology to the point where vast quantities of information are everywhere available at a moment's notice has taken many computer people by complete surprise. Today's on-line information systems in no way resemble yesterday's manual procedures, and many of the people involved with them lack the conceptual foundation that would allow them to assess the societal impact of the new technology. In short, it is not a matter of knowing

Societal impact of information technology

* Extract from the proceedings of an Online Conferences Ltd. conference and the subsequently published *Transnational Data Regulation: The Realities* (1979).

about and understanding recent advances in computers and telecommunications—technical people are very good at that kind of thing. It is, simply stated, that we are not exactly sure of what is being done with the new technology or of where the advances being made will eventually lead us. Clearly, the end result in both cases may be the same or very similar. Like surfers in a busy ocean, society is riding a swell of computer and telecommunications technology, and we would simply like to know the direction we are heading in and where we will land.

If, in fact, the social impact of computers and telecommunications technology is now—or will become—a problem to modern society, then a feasible solution is the creation of a generation of generalists, who know both computer technology and its societal impact. They would enable us to enjoy the fruits of the information explosion and to take full advantage of the versatility of modern computers.

Erosion of personal privacy and diminution of individual liberty

Annoying dislocations invariably accompany emerging technology. For instance, one can imagine the plight of the blacksmith in the early 1900s after the widespread acceptance of the motor vehicle. However, a new type of dislocation is associated with information technology: it involves the erosion of personal privacy and the diminution of individual liberty. This is perhaps the most significant problem to be solved by our hypothetical generation of generalists, and time to assess the problem is clearly in short supply.

Reasons for regulation

We simply do not have time to wait for the development of generalists, however, and so it falls upon the shoulders of today's organizations to protect privacy and insure liberty as part of their normal recordkeeping activity. Many European countries have already passed laws governing the transborder flow of information in order to protect the domain of their citizens. Obviously, there are other reasons for regulating the flow of data, which may very well affect the manner in which many multinational companies do business.

Regulation of technology

Essentially, we are talking about regulating technology—in this case, data flow through the use of computer and telecommunications technology. Other technologies, such as various forms of transportation, have been regulated in the past and are regulated today. However, this does not automatically imply that computers must be regulated as well. In fact, such regulation may turn out to be ineffective because advanced technology may provide a means of circumventing it. Considering the pace of advances in computer and telecommunications technology, staying one step ahead of current legislation does not provide even a small challenge.

PRINCIPLES OF REGULATION

One way of looking at regulation is as the administration of society in the interest of its citizens. As a procedural technique, regulation is customarily regarded as being developed on either an *a priori* or an *a posteriori* basis. Development on an a priori basis involves a determination of rights and activities that should be protected and the subsequent enactment of regulations that should in fact protect the specified rights and activities. In short, adverse consequences are determined on a hypothetico-deductive basis, and laws are passed with the ultimate objective of preventing the consequences from occurring. Development on an a posteriori basis involves the identification of rights and activities that have been abused, from a regulatory point of view, and the subsequent enactment of laws that would forestall the widespread occurrence of these abuses. In short, adverse conditions are determined on an empirico-inductive basis, and the ultimate effect of the conditions are predicted. Laws are then passed to prevent the consequences from occurring.

Development of regulation

Another aspect of the situation concerns the manner in which the desired conditions are obtained. One approach involves the creation of a *controlling agency* to govern an activity that could result in undesirable consequences. Licenses are issued, and only those persons or organizations that have secured a license may engage in the activity—a driver's license, for example, would fall into this category. Thus, the controlling agency achieves enforcement by establishing requirements for obtaining a license, by handling complaints and violations, and by performing investigatory work. Both the regulations and the controlling agency are commonly established by one act; this is known as the *omnibus approach*. The use of a controlling agency is normally associated with legislation determined on an a priori basis.

Controlling agency

A second approach is to enact laws that make certain types of activities illegal and to establish, either explicitly or implicitly, corresponding penalties for infringement. This approach, which is essentially self-enforcing, requires a minimum level of government intervention and is enforced through the *judicial process*. Inherently flexible, this ap-

Judicial approach

proach is normally associated with legislation determined on an a posteriori basis.

KEY FACTORS IN DATA REGULATION

One of the beneficial aspects of the present concern over data regulation is that it places the person about whom data are recorded in proper perspective. Whereas such a person may **Data subject** be the object in an information system, he or she is regarded as the subject in data regulation. This usage of the word *subject* is intended to imply that a person should in fact have some control over the storage of relevant information.

More specifically, the *subject* is the person, natural or **Beneficial user** legal, about whom data are stored. The *beneficial user* is the organization or individual for whom processing is performed, and the *agency* is the computing system in which the processing is performed. In many cases, the beneficial user **Agency** and the agency are members of the same organization. In fact, the subject, beneficial user, and agency may all be part of the same organization. In most cases, however, this will not be the case. For example, the agency may be a service company, and the subject may be a creditor.

In general, the beneficial user benefits from the data processed and has some control over the manner and time span in which the processing is performed. The agency need not be aware of the end use of the data or of how and when the processing is performed.

The heart of the issue is *data protection,* which normally refers to the protection of rights of individuals. While the **Questions of privacy** concept may also apply to groups of individuals, such as **and liberty** organizations or nations, the individual aspect of the issue also raises questions of privacy and liberty. Clearly, *privacy* refers to the claim of persons to determine when, how, and to what extent information about them is disclosed. However, it is also important to realize that it refers to freedom from intrusion and to freedom of thought, choice, and action. Thus, the notion of privacy noticeably extends beyond the control of informational resources.

CONSIDERATIONS IN DATA REGULATION

One of the primary objectives in regulating data flow is to protect against the negative consequences of modern information technology. Thus, data regulation can be viewed as the balancing of the freedoms and rights of the individual with the common interest of society. This process, normally interpreted as the stabilizing of information technology through the use of legal procedures, has in itself negative consequences; that is, laws and tariffs may seriously disrupt the flow of information upon which modern society is dependent. In fact, many people feel that the free international flow of information is a fundamental aspect of a comprehensive human rights program. **Stabilizing information technology**

Some countries resist the free flow of information across their borders because that information may erode their authority and control over their citizens. Others are concerned about the erosion of culture and traditional values. Still others are concerned about an increasing dependence on foreign information systems. The preceding discussion gives a flavor of the conditions that presently exist, which are covered in detail in Chapters 5 and 6. **Existing conditions**

PRACTICAL ISSUES IN DATA REGULATION

Although computers and modern information systems have not created the human rights issue, it is important to recognize that one of the basic methods of sustaining human rights is nevertheless achieved through the free flow of information. However, considerations of human rights, freedom of expression, and the invasion of privacy must be kept separate from the technical factors involved. Information technology can only provide a means of protecting privacy and promoting the unrestricted flow of information across international boundaries. **Human rights**

The substance of privacy laws effectively determines that the technical means of achieving privacy in information systems be commensurate with the level of risk involved. Thus, the level of security provided by an information system can be expected to depend upon the sensitivity of the data. Clearly, the cost of obtaining restricted data through the penetration of an information system would not exceed the value of the information. In fact, even though the data may not be sensitive, the manner in which they are used may constitute an invasion of privacy. **Cost of achieving privacy**

Practically speaking, a clear definition of what constitutes private and personal information is lacking. As a substitute for a sensitivity ordering of personal data, there is a general belief that more sensitive data are positively correlated with **Sensitive data** the degree of seriousness of an invasion of privacy and the need for data protection. (Relatively unimportant data such as family status, employment, education, and hobbies have low sensitivity, and it is not generally regarded as serious if they are revealed. On the other hand, credit and other financial data have high sensitivity, and it is more serious if they are revealed because it may result in lawsuits, etc.)

In providing data protection in an information system environment, two controls are particularly important:

Controls for data protection

1. Measures must exist to protect against unauthorized new uses of data. (This refers to the merging of files and the exchange of files between agencies.)
2. Data protection must exist independently of the agency and its location. (This refers to files that are transferred to other jurisdictions with confidence that data-protection laws are complementary.)

Clearly, the most important aspect of controls over the use of data is whether they are enforceable; this is precisely why it is important to deal in general principles. As mentioned previously, advanced technology may provide the means of circumventing detailed regulations.

DATA VAULTS, DATA HAVENS, AND RELATED CONCEPTS

Misuse of information

As the cost of computer networks and associated data processing decreases, there is a growing concern over the misuse of information by businesses and government. Data vaults and data havens are concepts employed to prevent the misuse or even the use of information. While these notions are not of an immediate or long-range concern in data regulation, they provide important background material.

Data vault

A *data vault* is an operational situation wherein data from one country are stored and processed in another country in order to obtain special protection for the parties involved. For example, a national company may assure its clients that personal information is stored in a foreign country beyond the reach of national authorities. Such storage constitutes a data vault when its data-protection laws guard against disclosure.

A *data haven* is an operational situation wherein data from one country are stored and processed in another country because the latter's data protection laws are lenient and permit disclosures that would be illegal in the originating country. This is a major reason for the data protection laws that have been passed by several countries. Through the routine use of international telecommunications facilities, it is convenient to do processing in a foreign data processing center. Although national data protection laws apply to the beneficial user and effectively govern storage and processing in a foreign country, it is difficult to enforce such laws when the records and the processing facility cannot be physically inspected. Moreover, "new" use of information may take place in the foreign location, such that original ownership of the data becomes significant.

Data haven

Both data vaults and data havens can be used to secure a competitive business advantage. A data vault can serve to instill trust in a business-client relationship and provide economic benefit to the country in which the agency is located. If the subject, the beneficial user, and the agency are all located in the same country, then that country has furthered its own economic cause through the use of effective data protection laws. In an analogous but exactly opposite manner, a data processing service organization located in a country with lenient data protection laws can serve as a data haven for credit reporting, subscription processing, and credit card services. The client, in such a case, normally volunteers a certain amount of information commensurate with the service provided, and this information is commonly used for other purposes.

Reasons for data vaults and havens

SOME INSIGHTS INTO THE ECONOMICS AND POLITICS OF DATA REGULATION

Although the preservation of individual freedom may be an important motivating factor behind data protection legislation, it is by no means the only factor, and it may not even be the primary factor. In fact, many people feel that the main reasons for data regulation are economic and political. This section gives a brief overview of economic and political issues. The subject is covered further in Chapter 6.

Economics and politics

Without attempting to be specific about the issues and parties involved, it can be equitably stated that the actors in the data regulation scenario are divided into two camps: those who favor regulation and those who do not. The parties favoring regulation state that they do so for economic, po-

Actors in data regulation scenario are divided into two camps

litical, or libertarian reasons. The parties who oppose regulation also give economic, political, or libertarian justifications for their viewpoint, but their emphasis is primarily economic.

Some of the reasons that have been forwarded for favoring the regulation of transborder data flow are summarized in the following list:

Reasons for favoring the regulation of transborder data flow

1. Use of foreign service bureaus constitutes an economic drain on a country. Introducing restrictions on transborder data transfer is an effective means of protecting national service bureaus against foreign competition.
2. Regulation of transborder data transfer can be used as a means of establishing a national computer industry, by restricting the hardware and software that can be developed or marketed in a country.
3. Transborder data regulation can be used as a means of imposing taxes and other sanctions on transborder data traffic.
4. Transborder data regulation can be used to reduce the level of dependence of one country on another country and to permit a country to retain control over its information technology.
5. A general fear exists that governments will invade individual privacy unless there is some form of data protection. Clearly, this fear is much stronger in some countries than others because of the occurrence of historical events. In the United States, the courts are used to uphold privacy protection laws. In Europe, data protection laws covering a broad range of potential risks are used because the courts are less likely to oppose government intrusion.

In addition, there is also a general belief, held primarily by some European groups, that unrestricted transborder data flow will create a technological dependence on the countries that lead in telecommunications technology.

Some of the reasons that have been stated for opposing data regulation are summarized as follows:

1. Different countries may adopt different data protection laws, thereby increasing the cost of compliance and

obstructing the timely flow of information. Tariffs may increase operating costs.

2. Data protection laws may result in restraint of foreign competition, thus causing increased operating costs and lower profit margins. This would result in higher costs to users and a possible deterioration of service through the use of alternate facilities.

3. Restricting the free flow of technology will hamper the economic growth of countries, since no nation is completely self-sufficient with regard to information technology.

4. Restrictive transborder data flow regulations can disrupt the internal operation of many multinational companies. Computing facilities and data files would have to be replicated, and the use of centralized planning data bases could be severely curtailed. The level of customer service would be reduced.

5. Certain types of data regulation would result in non-optimal solutions to data processing problems. For example, the use of a computer in a foreign country as a backup facility might not be possible with data regulation, thereby increasing the effective cost of data processing.

6. Nations in our modern global society are technically and economically interdependent, and many services, such as reservation, production scheduling, and shipment, are more efficiently and effectively performed by independent and possibly private organizations. Replacement costs for the services would be high and probably would result in ineffective service.

Reasons for opposing the regulation of transborder data flow

Along with these reasons goes the underlying attitude that communications and computer technology are national resources that must be balanced with existing natural resources.

SUMMARY

The widespread use of computer-based information systems represents a virtual revolution in that computer and communications technology are combined to provide a capability whereby vast quantities of information are available at a moment's notice. The benefits of modern information technology must be weighed against the social, economic, and political concerns that can be generated as undesirable by-products of the advanced technology. Clearly, it is in the domain of modern organizations to balance the advantages and disadvantages of these informational capabilities.

One means of controlling the impact of information technology is to regulate it. Data regulation can be determined on an a priori or an a posteriori basis depending on whether the laws are based on a prediction of events that might occur or as a result of events that have occurred, respectively. The resulting data protection can subsequently be implemented by a controlling agency and a licensing procedure, or through the judicial process.

Three parties or groups are involved in data regulation: the subject about whom data are recorded, the beneficial user for whom processing is performed, and the agency where the processing is done. The heart of the issue is data protection, which refers to the rights of individuals. One of the primary objectives in regulating data flow is to protect against the negative consequences of information technology, so that data regulation can be regarded as the balancing of the rights of the individual against the needs of society. Two aspects of data protection are particularly important: protection against unauthorized new uses of data and protection that exists independently of where the data are processed. Two operational concepts employed to prevent the misuse or use of data are data vaults and data havens.

Many people feel that the main reasons for data regulation are economic and political. Thus, individual freedom may be an important reason for data protection legislation, but it is by no means the only reason.

IMPORTANT TERMS AND CONCEPTS

The reader should be familiar with the following terms and concepts:

Agency
A posteriori development of legislation
A priori development of legislation
Beneficial user
Controlling agency
Data haven
Data protection

Data vault
Human rights
Judicial process
Level of risk
Negative consequence of information technology
New use of data
Omnibus approach
Subject

READINGS AND REFERENCES

Benjamin, A. A. Privacy, security, and responsibility. In *Transnational Data Regulation: The Realities,* pp. 2–8. Uxbridge, England: Online Conferences Ltd., 1979.

Bing, J. Transborder data flows: Some legal issues and possible effects on business practices. In *Transnational Data Regulation: The Realities,* pp. 16–27. Uxbridge, England: Online Conferences Ltd., 1979.

Dunn, N. Us vs. them. *Computer Decisions* (February 1979), pp. 24–30.

Eger, J. M. Alliance for world communications. *Transnational Data Regulation.* In *Transnational Data Regulation: The Realities.* pp. 34–39. Uxbridge, England: Online Conferences Ltd., 1979.

Freese, J. Transborder data flow: Should it be regulated? Pro. *Computerworld* (October 30, 1978), p. 62.

Hirsch, P. Europe's privacy laws—Fear of inconsistency. *Datamation* (February 1979), pp. 85–88.

Kirchner, J. United States data policy to stipulate open data flow. *Computerworld* (February 19, 1979), p. 1.

Langhorne, R. W. Transborder data flow: Should it be regulated? Con. *Computerworld* (October 30, 1978), p. 63.

Miller, A. R. *The Assault on Privacy: Computers, Data Banks, and Dossiers.* Ann Arbor: The University of Michigan Press, 1971.

Transnational Data Regulation: The Realities. Uxbridge, England: Online Conferences Ltd., 1979.

Turn, R. Implementation of Privacy and Security Requirements in Trans-National Data Processing Systems. In *Transnational Data Regulation: The Realities,* pp. 114–132. Uxbridge, England: Online Conferences Ltd., 1979.

2

NOTES ON LIBERTY, FREEDOM, AND RIGHTS

*Freedom in general may be defined as the absence of obstacles
to the realization of desires.*

BERTRAND RUSSELL

In discussing the limits to the authority of society over the individual, John Stuart Mill wisely pointed out in 1859:

John Stuart Mill

> Though society is not founded on a contract, and though no good purpose is answered by inventing a contract in order to deduce social obligations from it, every one who receives the protection of society owes a return for the benefit, and the fact of living in society renders it indispensable that each should be bound to observe a certain line of conduct towards the rest. This conduct consists, first, in not injuring the interests of one another; or rather certain interests, which, either by express legal provision or by tacit understanding, ought to be considered as rights; and secondly, in each person's bearing his share (to be fixed on some equitable principle) of the labours and sacrifices incurred for defending the society or its members from injury and molestation. These conditions society is justified in enforcing, at all costs to those who endeavour to withhold fulfilment.[1]

Mill's observations aptly set the stage for a brief discussion of individual liberty and effectively initiate an analysis of several key relevant topics ranging from the state, law, and morality to personal right and choice.

[1] Mill, J. S. *On Liberty* (Published in R. M. Hutchins, ed., *Great Books of the Western World*, Volume 43, pp. 302–303. Encyclopaedia Britannica, Inc., Chicago, 1952).

It would be inappropriate to imply from the quotation that individuals should not be concerned with the affairs of other individuals—except in their own self-interest. Society is too dynamic and interdependent for that. On the other hand, an individual is most interested in his or her own well-being. One's personal self-knowledge is paramount, and the interference of society, except in extreme cases, is likely to be inappropriate.

Interpretation

Clearly, societal regulation is not fundamentally intended to restrain the actions of individuals, but rather, to help them. Government should provide benefits—either directly or indirectly—to individuals, instead of requiring that they acquire a corresponding service for themselves. The areas of health, education, trade, crime management, and transportation are obvious examples of societal concerns. While individuals are not accountable to society for their actions, traditional forms of social and legal punishment have resulted from certain individual actions that invade the domain of others.

Societal concerns

The infringement by persons upon the interests of others does not alone justify the interference of society. In fact, Mill's *Principle of Individual Liberty* promotes a single purpose:

> That principle is, that the sole end for which mankind are warranted, individually or collectively, in interfering with the liberty of action of any of their number, is self-protection. That the only purpose for which power can be rightfully exercised over any member of a civilised community, against his will, is to prevent harm to others.[2]

Individual liberty

Other popular objections to government interference are:

1. Actions are better performed by individuals than by government.
2. In cases where government performance excels over individual performance, actions are preferably performed by individuals for their own self-betterment.
3. Government interference into individual affairs adds unnecessarily to its power.

Classic struggle between liberty and authority

The preceding discussion represents the classic struggle between liberty and authority.

---

[2] Mill, *Principle of Individual Liberty,* op. cit., p. 271.

Concepts such as *self-government* provide neither a solution to the problem of liberty v. authority, nor a clear representation of the problem. The notion of *tyranny of the majority* means that individuals who exercise power are not always the same individuals over whom power is exercised. The situation is summarized by Mill:

Tyranny of the majority

> But reflecting persons perceived that when society is itself the tyrant—society collectively over the separate individuals who compose it—its means of tyrannising are not restricted to the acts which it may do by the hands of its political functionaries. Society can and does execute its own mandates: and if it issues wrong mandates instead of right, or any mandates at all in things with which it ought not to meddle, it practises a social tyranny more formidable than many kinds of political oppression, since, though not usually upheld by such extreme penalties, it leaves fewer means of escape, penetrating much more deeply into the details of life, and enslaving the soul itself. Protection, therefore, against the tyranny of the magistrate is not enough: there needs protection also against the tyranny of the prevailing opinion and feeling; against the tendency of society to impose, by other means than civil penalties, its own ideas and practices as rules of conduct on those who dissent from them; to fetter the development, and, if possible, prevent the formation, of any individuality not in harmony with its ways, and compels all characters to fashion themselves upon the model of its own. There is a limit to the legitimate interference of collective opinion with individual independence: and to find that limit, and maintain it against encroachment, is as indispensable to a good condition of human affairs, as protection against political despotism.[3]

FREEDOM

As a social concept, *freedom* refers to the relationship between individuals in an interpersonal environment. An individual is usually considered to be free when his or her condition exists without coercion or constraint imposed by another individual. Thus, a free individual can select goals and appropriate alternatives, and is not restricted in thought or action by the will or presence of another person. In a political sense, an individual is free when he or she is not restricted, as covered above, by the state or other authority.

Freedom is lack of coercion or constraint

The above notion of freedom can be enlarged somewhat

[3] Mill op. cit., p. 269.

by considering the "conditions" under which actions can be performed and the "means" by which they are executed. The current thinking is that natural or societal conditions, defined in the broadest possible sense, constitute constraints on the individual's ability to establish goals and to select among alternate courses of action; moreover, any knowledge that aids one in using existing conditions to realize purposes increases one's freedom. In addition, freedom is determined according to whether we have the power to achieve a goal or execute a selected course of action. Therefore, the absence of the means or power to do something is equivalent to the absence of freedom to do it. To sum up, freedom necessarily entails the following conditions:

Establish goals and select among alternate courses of action

Power to achieve a goal

1. The absence of coercion or restraint in any form by an individual, the state, or other authority that would prevent an individual from selecting specific goals and taking certain courses of action.
2. The absence of natural or societal conditions that would prevent the attainment of specific objectives.
3. The possession of the power to or the means of achieving a specific objective.

Conditions for freedom

The conditions effectively equate *to be free to* with *to be able to*. They emphasize that the absence of the power and social means of achieving a selected goal is not necessarily restricted to simple cases wherein one person imposes restrictions on the activities of another.

A key word in the concept of freedom is *coercion*. In addition to the commonly known behavioral forms of restraint, coercion also incorporates the concepts of manipulation and control and of the possession of relevant information with which to make an informed choice. For example, an authoritarian society might manipulate and control the minds of individuals by governing the information and activities to which they are exposed. Through various forms of propaganda and conditioning, individuals can be made to favor the alternatives that their authority wants them to favor without proper consideration of other alternatives.

Coercion

Coercion also includes the activity of an authority that constrains an individual from making a proper choice among available alternatives because knowledge or understanding of certain alternatives is restricted.

In both cases, a person, including the notion of a legal per-

Information and freedom

son, may not be aware of the existence of obstructions of freedom. Information extends the capacity for freedom of activity, and a lack of freedom generally restricts that capacity. Although a lack of possible alternatives for choice is not explicitly regarded as a lack of freedom, the absence of a suitable alternative is usually regarded as a restraint of the freedom of choice.

Negative freedom

The *freedom from* coercion or constraint by others is commonly known as *negative freedom*. The preceding discussion was primarily concerned with negative freedom, and popular issues, such as personal privacy, frequently involve this aspect of the subject matter. *Positive freedom,* on the other

Positive freedom

hand, is associated with the process of acting on one's own behalf. Commonly known examples are freedom from want, freedom from fear, freedom of speech, freedom in the choice of employer, and freedom of movement.

In most modern societies, freedom is usually associated with social, economic, and political power—that is, some individuals or organizations, due to their unique position or control over resources, can limit the range of alternatives of

Power and freedom

other individuals. Depriving individuals of the means to attain a chosen alternative is a form of coercion; it is used in order to force compliance with social, economic, or political demands. Thus, a positive freedom, such as freedom from want, is effectively negative freedom. The existence of unequal power simply means that those individuals also possess unequal freedom of choice.

Choice

Thus, the notions of freedom and power are directly related to an individual's opportunity for making full choice in a society. Clearly, negative and positive freedom serve as a basis for the existence of choice, so that a system in which power is distributed is also one in which there exist wide possibilities for individual choice.

THE STATE, LAW, AND MORALITY

The essence of government can be regarded as the formalization of an underlying set of laws of nature. The executive responsibility of government usually entails three classes of activity:

1. *Legislative activity:* establishing the desired rules of conduct.

Governmental activity

2. *Judicial activity:* applying the rules of conduct to specific occurrences of appropriate events.

3. *Penal activity:* sanctioning those individuals who have obeyed the rules of conduct.

A society is commonly regarded as a *state* if it contains a centralized agency for performing these three activities. Historically, the state performed two essential functions:

1. Maintenance of law and order
2. Defense against external enemies

Functions of state

Transl ted into modern ideas, the state's functions involve the welfare of individual citizens and the survival of the state as a sovereign entity.

A collection of people who interact, cooperate, and communicate is regarded as a *society.* A society will persist only if it has generally accepted rules of conduct. The rules need not be formalized in order for a society to survive. However, when formalized in the form of a government, rules are commonly known as *laws.* A collection of people with the same government is called a *country.*

Society

Laws are a product of a sovereign state. (Such laws are regarded as *proper laws,* as compared to the *private regulations* of a family, club, or enterprise.) Most laws are historically or fundamentally based on *natural law,* a system of rights considered common to mankind. In modern times, natural law serves only as a standard of guidance when one is faced with conflicting ideologies. Natural implies that a law is not legal, whereas *positive law* is conferred by the state and enforced through official sanction. For rather obvious reasons, positive law is very precise, while natural law tends to be regarded as the broad moral consensus of the people. On the whole, many people believe that positive law is difficult or impossible to enforce if it runs contrary to natural law.

Natural law

Positive law

Although there are no absolutely valid and unquestionable moral principles, some rights can be considered natural in the sense that they are moral and not guaranteed by law. These rights are possessed by all mankind and do not generally depend upon membership in a particular society. This class of rights is sometimes referred to as *human rights.*

Natural rights

OBLIGATION, LIBERTY, AND SOCIAL COST

The state has a right to the obedience of those for whom it performs services. However, the existence of a law that is contrary to natural law is sufficient reason for some indivi-

Obedience

duals to disregard that law. On the other hand, many people give obedience to the state either out of habit or because it is reasonable to do so, without due regard to questions of morality and utilitarianism.

Looking at political obedience more closely, the question, Why should one show obedience to the state? is answered by one of three classes of theories: intrinsic, extrinsic, or organic. *Intrinsic theories* include such reasons as:

1. It has always been done *(traditionalism)*.
2. God has commanded us to do so *(divine right)*.

Theories of obedience

3. Authority is vested in the best people *(aristocracy)*.

Extrinsic theories cover such reasons as:

1. People have indirectly contracted to do so *(social contract)*.
2. It is necessary for the general welfare of society as a whole *(utilitarianism)*.

Intrinsic and extrinsic theories implicitly view the people and the state as fundamentally different entities; the citizens are distinct from and subordinate to the state. In an *organic theory,* the state represents the "better selves" of the people.

The notion of an absolute choice between obedience and resistance is perhaps not realistic, but it does reflect a con-

Negative and positive liberty

Social cost

cern for liberty or "doing what one wants to do." The absence of interference (negative liberty) and the ability to do what one really wants to do (positive liberty) must ultimately be based on the *social cost* of maintaining obedience. Clearly, the cost of regulation may represent an inordinately heavy economic burden that may ultimately offset any benefits derived therefrom.

RIGHT AND CHOICE

Hart claimed that if there exists any natural right at all, it is the equal right of all people to be free.[4] Berlin expounded on the subject:

I wish to be a subject, not an object; to be moved by reasons, by conscious purposes which are my own, not by causes which af-

---

[4] Hart, H. L. A. Are there any natural rights? In *Political Philosophy,* edited by A. Quinton, p. 53. Oxford, England: Oxford University Press, 1967. Courtesy of Oxford University Press.

fect me, as it were, from outside. I wish to be somebody, not nobody; a doer—deciding, not being decided for, self-directed and not acted upon by external nature or by other men as if I were a thing, or an animal, or a slave incapable of playing a human role, that is, of conceiving goals and policies of my own and realizing them.[5]

Natural right to be free

The term *right* falls somewhere between law and morality and is commonly associated with the words *droit, deritto,* and *Recht,* frequently used by continental jurists.

There exists a segment of that which we loosely call *morality* that contains principles governing the degree to which one individual can determine how another individual can act. In this sense, the notion of right is accompanied by such familiar notions as justice, fairness, and obligation.

Right as morality

Clearly, right, obligation, and duty are correlates. For example, an individual has a right to personal autonomy. That right can be violated through a computer-based information system. An obligation to maintain personal autonomy is thereby incurred by the agency and beneficial user, and they have a duty to provide an appropriate level of data protection. Even though a subject stands to benefit by the existence of such a system, the subject continues to possess the right to personal autonomy, and it is the duty of agency and beneficial user to maintain that right. A common example is the right of animals and babies not to be ill-treated, and our duty to provide proper treatment.

Personal autonomy

The existence of a right can be used to limit an individual's freedom of choice. Through an irreversible promissory act, an individual *B* agrees to perform a particular task for individual *A*. *A* has a moral claim (i.e., a right) upon *B* to have *B* perform the task. However, *A* can waive the claim and release *B* from the obligation. Thus, *A* can act in such a way as to limit *B*'s freedom of choice. For example, an individual (*A*) waives his or her claim to personal autonomy, to some extent, when filling out an application for a credit card or a mortgage loan and thereby relieves the granting organization (*B*) of its social obligation.

Right as a limitation of freedom of choice

The logic of rights becomes more apparent when a third party is involved—as in the example of subject, agency, and beneficial user. In this case, the beneficial user explicitly or implicitly guarantees to the subject that a certain level of

---

[5] Berlin, I. Concepts of liberty, op. cit., p. 149. Courtesy of Oxford University Press.

Logic of rights: subject, agency, and beneficial user

data protection will be maintained. The agency guarantees to the beneficial user that the subject's rights will be maintained. Even though the subject is the person who will benefit from the data protection, the agency has an obligation to the beneficial user to maintain the level of data protection, and, correspondingly, the beneficial user possesses a right to that protection. Thus, the beneficial user has a claim on the agency and can release the agency from the obligation. The identity of the party who stands to benefit from the obligation (i.e., the subject) is determined by considering what will happen if the duty is not performed. The identity of the party who possesses the right (i.e., the party to whom something is owed) is determined by analyzing the previous transactions.

Rights are generally classed as special or general. A *special right* results from a transaction among individuals and can take one of several forms:

Special right

1. A promise to do or not to do something.
2. One individual authorizes another individual to act on his or her behalf.
3. A mutually restricted obligation whereby individuals agree to cooperate in a venture and possess the correlative right to obedience. Thus, one individual's expectations of another individual's behavior is governed by the nature of their relationship.

Clearly, special rights can take a wide variety of forms. Collectively they provide justification for one person's interference with the freedom of another person.

A *general right* is an assertion offered defensively when interference with one's freedom is planned, threatened, or expected. It is a moral justification that determines how an-

General right

other person will act—for example, "he will not interfere," or "I can say what I please."

Hart summarized the distinction between general and special rights:

> But there are of course striking differences between such defensive general rights and special rights. (1) General rights do not arise out of any special relationship or transaction between men. (2) General rights are not rights which are peculiar to those who have them but are rights which all men capable of choice have in the absence of those special conditions which give rise to special

rights. (3) General rights have as correlatives obligations not to interfere to which everyone else is subject and not merely the parties to some special relationship or transaction, though of course they will often be asserted when some particular persons threaten to interfere as a moral objection to that interference.[6]

It follows that rights are effectively "owned" by individuals, so that the obligation refers to both the behavior of individuals and the behavior that can be expected of other individuals.

Rights are owned by individuals

SUMMARY

Considerations of the limitations of the authority of society over the individual are well steeped in history and are prominent in the writings of John Stuart Mill and other political philosophers. Modern society is dynamic and interdependent, and some forms of social regulation are fundamental to everyday existence. In fact, traditional forms of social and legal punishment have resulted from actions that invade the domain of others. These concepts are embodied in Mill's *Principle of Individual Liberty*.

Freedom is a social concept that refers to the relationship among individuals in an interpersonal environment. An individual who is free can select goals, appropriate alternatives, and is not restricted in thought or action by the will or presence of another person. Important considerations are the conditions under which actions would be performed and the means by which they are performed. A key word in the concept of freedom is *coercion*. In general, freedom from coercion is embodied in two concepts: negative freedom and positive freedom.

The existence of a centralized agency for performing legislative, judicial, and penal activities in an organized society is commonly regarded as *state*. Laws are historically derived from natural law, which is a system of rights common to mankind. Legal laws are known as positive laws, which are conferred by the state and enforced through official sanction. Key concepts related to the existence of a state are political obligation, the notion of liberty, and social cost.

Rights are owned by individuals and refer to individual behavior (what a person can do) and the behavior that can be

[6] Hart, op. cit., p. 64. Courtesy of Oxford University Press.

expected of others (what rights a person has). The existence of a right can be used to limit an individual's freedom of choice and has as its correlates obligation and duty.

IMPORTANT TERMS AND CONCEPTS

The reader should be familiar with the following terms and concepts:

Aristocracy	Organic theory
Coercion	Penal activity
Divine right	Positive freedom
Duty	Positive law
Extrinsic theory	Positive liberty
Freedom	Power
General right	Principle of individual liberty
Intrinsic theory	Right
Judicial activity	Social contract
Laws of nature	Social cost
Legislative activity	Societal regulation
Liberty	Society
Means	Special right
Natural law	State
Natural right	Traditionalism
Negative freedom	Tyranny of the majority
Negative liberty	Utilitarianism
Obligation	

READINGS AND REFERENCES

Berlin, I. Concepts of liberty. In *Political Philosophy,* edited by A. Quinton, pp. 141–152. Oxford, England: Oxford University Press, 1967.

Bronowski, J. *Science and Human Values.* New York: Harper & Row, 1965.

Edwards, P., ed. Freedom. In *The Encyclopedia of Philosophy,* vol. 3, pp. 221–115. New York: Free Press, 1967.

Hart, H. L. A. Are there any natural rights? In *Political Philosophy,* edited by A. Quinton, pp. 53–66. Oxford, England: Oxford University Press, 1967.

Mill, J. S. On liberty. In *Great Books of the Western World,* edited by R. M. Hutchins and M. Adler, vol. 43. Chicago: Encyclopaedia Brittanica Educational Corp., 1952.

———. *Utilitarianism, On Liberty, Essay on Bentham,* edited by Mary Warnock. New York: New American Library, 1974.

Quinton, A., ed. *Political Philosophy.* Oxford, England: Oxford University Press, 1967.

Skinner, B.F. *Beyond Freedom and Dignity.* New York: Alfred A. Knopf, 1971.

3

INFORMATION TECHNOLOGY

This advent of computer and communications technology is causing a quiet revolution to occur in the field of information. It is quiet because the signs of changes are subtle and not always visible. It is a revolution because the rate of change is very rapid.

> NATIONAL INFORMATION POLICY
> Report to the President of
> the United States

Information technology is informally defined as the effective use of computer hardware, software, data communications technology, and information that have been integrated in a systems environment in such a manner as to have a synergistic effect on the performance of the various components. Information technology does not exist in a vacuum, and its power and capability are normally available through modern organizational structures.

Synergistic effect

Information technology is a dynamic subject, and its various components are constantly being restructured as events occur in the real world. Individual and organizational behavior are also constantly changing. Thus, the relationship among an organization, an individual, and information technology represents a dynamic system that must be monitored constantly. Information technology is growing rapidly; if its widespread use is allowed to increase without due consideration of the end results, undesirable consequences could occur. Such consequences could be the incremental result of independent decisions by well-intentioned managers and administrators.

Rapid growth of information technology

On the other hand, most organizations—including various forms of government—require a large amount of informa-

Information needs

tion in order to sustain efficient and effective day-to-day operations and to plan for the future. Also, in many cases, a large quantity of information is required to satisfy government regulations.

Because of the widespread need for informational resources, rapid technological advances have been made in the computer field, resulting in more effective and efficient in-

Technological advances

formation systems. However, this situation presents somewhat of a paradox for persons in advisory and policymaking positions. Clearly, it would be desirable to employ the most recently developed features in information technology, but there exists an ever-present danger that the technology would produce unwanted social side effects.

Computer specialists can provide a means of storing, communicating, and accessing information, and it is the role of the administrator to specify informational requirements and control the use of relevant information. One method of re-

Regulation

solving the dilemma is to regulate the development of information technology. This task may be impossible. However, if such regulation is possible, it could produce undesirable side effects, such as a lessening in the rate of technological growth.

This chapter presents the background material on information technology that is needed in order to place its constit-

Objectives

uent components in proper perspective. It also emphasizes that the reasons for using a computer system do not simply involve the replacement of clerical data processing tasks——even though data processing is indeed an important function. An equally important function is to provide insight into

Insight and information systems

the processes of problem-solving and decisionmaking, and data analysis, planning, and controlling. Insight requires information, which is where the concept of an information system comes in. Information technology provides the means of establishing an efficient and effective information system.

INFORMATION SYSTEMS

An *information system* is an organized collection of computer hardware components, computer software, application programs, data, and operational procedures. It is specifically configured and managed to support the operations, decision-

Relationship among information system components

making, and planning functions of an organization. The various components are represented in Figure 3–1, where the relationship among the components is suggested by the rela-

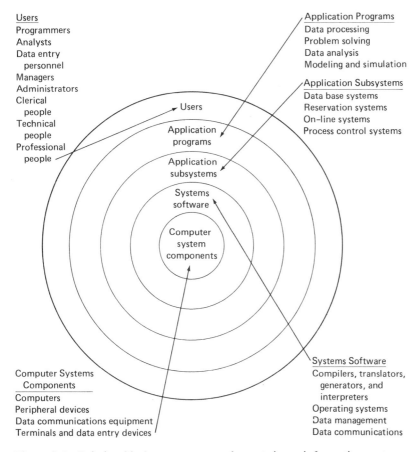

Users
Programmers
Analysts
Data entry
  personnel
Managers
Administrators
Clerical
  people
Technical
  people
Professional
  people

Application Programs
Data processing
Problem solving
Data analysis
Modeling and simulation

Application Subsystems
Data base systems
Reservation systems
On-line systems
Process control systems

Users

Application programs

Application subsystems

Systems software

Computer system components

Computer Systems
  Components
Computers
Peripheral devices
Data communications equipment
Terminals and data entry devices

Systems Software
Compilers, translators,
  generators, and
  interpreters
Operating systems
Data management
Data communications

Figure 3-1. Relationship between system elements in an information system.

tionship of the concentric circles. As the figure illustrates, an information system consists of the following elements:

Computer system components
Systems software
Applications subsystems
Application programs
Users

Each element will be described in a separate section in this chapter; some general remarks will be made here without going into detail.

In the center of Figure 3-1, the hardware and software technology is very complex, and only a few people are actually involved in the associated developmental activity. Even though the impact of this highly technical work may be widespread, the number of people involved is nevertheless mini-

Number of people involved

mal. However, as we move away from the center of the figure, more people are involved with the specific hardware and software elements and the information system as a whole.

ORGANIZATIONAL FUNCTIONS

Modern viewpoint

In an organizational environment, an information system should store only the type and quantity of information needed for the various organizational functions. This modern viewpoint is more realistic than the outdated notion that an information system should store all forms of information that could possibly affect the present and future functioning of the organization.

Organization as an information processor

Another important consideration is that the organization functions as an information processor. Information is summarized and generalized as it moves downward in the organization. Patterns of information flow within an organization serve to maintain the power structure and promote effective decisionmaking, by providing the various levels of management or administration with the type and quantity of information that is needed. Clearly, top management deals with more general issues than do specialists, who require technical or detailed information for performing day-to-day activities.

Informational pyramid

The informational pyramid, shown in Figure 3–2, depicts the organization functions supported by an information system. Going from the top of the pyramid to the bottom, the various functions are:

Policy planning
Formulation of objectives and strategic plans
Planning and budgeting
Operational control and decisionmaking
Inquiry/response (on-line) systems
Data processing

Overall, the various organizational functions support the goal-setting, control, innovation, and intelligence requirements of complex organizations.

Data processing

The organizational function that requires the most detailed information is *data processing,* which performs the day-to-day transaction processing normally associated with the activities of the organization, such as payroll, accounts payable and receivable, and inventory control. In the case of some government agencies and many service organizations, data processing is the primary organizational function.

Inquiry/response systems are the next level in the pyramid. They incorporate on-line facilities for accessing information with traditional data processing functions. Through the use of a data base, telecommunications facilities, and appropriate software, a user can access the data base from a remote location, thereby providing rapid response to certain types of queries.

Inquiry/response systems

Moving up the pyramid in Figure 3-2, it is apparent that the administrative or managerial aspects of organizational activity are more closely integrated with the information system. Data processing and inquiry/response information are summarized at the next level for operational control and decisionmaking, and the process continues from there to include planning and budgeting, formulation of objectives and strategic planning, and lastly, policy planning. As one progresses closer to the top of the pyramid, it becomes increas-

Administration and management

Figure 3-2. Informational pyramid.

ingly more important that an information system match the specific characteristics of the organization.

COMPUTER SYSTEM COMPONENTS

The class of computer system components, which is frequently referred to as the "hardware system," normally contains the following equipment:

> Computers
> Peripheral devices
> Data communications equipment
> Terminals and data entry devices

Total computer system in perspective

Since the computer, per se, performs control and monitoring functions, it can be regarded as the "heart" of the computer system. Nevertheless, it may actually represent only a small fraction of the cost of a total computer system. In fact, computers have a relatively short life span (approximately five to seven years), whereas terminals and data entry devices last substantially longer. Moreover, there is customarily more concern in computer-installation management over data entry devices, because, as a general class of equipment, they affect a wider range of users on a day-to-day basis for an extended period of time.

Basic computer components

Computers. A computer performs the arithmetic, logical, and control functions of a computer system through a central processing unit and a main storage unit. The *central processing unit* operates under the direction of instructions held on a temporary basis in the *main storage unit,* which is a relatively high-speed storage device designed to hold instructions and data during processing but not for extended periods of time. Computers are generally classed as follows:

> *Microcomputers.* The central processing unit and the main storage unit of a microcomputer are fabricated on a few electronic chips. Microcomputers, which are relatively inexpensive, are used primarily for control and monitoring applications, in data entry and terminal/display devices, with small business or problem-solving machines, and in personal/hobby systems. Microcomputers do not in general contain facilities for general-purpose data processing and for information systems.

Minicomputers. A minicomputer is a general-purpose computer system normally dedicated to a single application or class of applications, which requires only a modest investment in time and money. Physically small in size, it usually does not require special environmental conditions. Typical minicomputer applications include: control special equipment such as bank cash machines, function as a network computer for a communication system, run scoreboards in a sports arena, collect laboratory data, provide access to a data base system, and serve as a small-business computer with full functional capability.

Medium-scale and large-scale computers. This is the expensive class of full-function computers requiring special environmental conditions and an in-house computer staff. Medium- and large-scale computers can support on-line systems and provide information systems support. These computers operate at high speeds and give a high number of computations per dollar, because of economy of scale. All types of applications are normally included in this class.

Classification of computers

The efficiency and effectiveness of a computer system depend upon the peripheral devices attached to it and upon the software used to control its operation.

Peripheral Devices. Hardware devices that are external to the computer per se, but supply necessary input, output, and mass storage functions, are referred to as *peripheral devices.* Typical peripheral devices are:

Line printers: Used to generate printed reports.

Card readers: Used to enter the contents of punched cards into the computer.

Magnetic tape units: Used for the mass storage of information on magnetic tape media.

Disk storage units: Used for the mass storage of information on direct-access media.

Also classed as peripheral devices are hardware units for a variety of physical media, such as optical character readers (including on- and off-line magnetic-ink character readers customarily used for check processing), micrographic reader/recorders, plotting devices, and paper-tape readers/punches, as well as the very large capacity mass-storage systems. A special class of peripheral devices is concerned with control

Peripheral devices

applications. In this class, the computer serves as the control mechanism, which is connected by a peripheral device to a physical apparatus. Typical cases are the control of temperature in a chemical process, the collection of laboratory test data, or the numerical control of a manufacturing process. Peripheral devices in this class are sensing units and analog/digital converters.

Data Communications Equipment. One of the most rapid growth areas in information technology involves the use of data communications equipment, which includes the following:

Telecommunications equipment

> *Data communications channels:* physical circuits, microwave circuits, and optical methods. This category is normally classed as public networks, private networks, and satellite systems.
>
> *Network processors:* front end processors, switching computers, and concentrators. This category usually involves the use of minicomputers for handling the communications aspects of a computer network.
>
> *Network equipment:* modems, multiplexers, polling devices, port sharing, and line-splitting devices. This category incorporates facilities for handling the physical processes of data communications.

Managers, administrators, and data processing personnel generally regard this class of computer hardware as the least understood aspect of information technology. This is unfortunate because data communications is an integral part of national and multinational computer systems and of distributed data processing systems. Through the use of data communications facilities, a user at a remote location can access the computer and obtain information at a moment's notice. In order to do so, other facilities are needed—such as appropriate software and a terminal device. However, the key point has been made. The remoteness of a user requires that special precautions be maintained for data protection since visual identity is not possible.

Remote access capability

Terminals and Data Entry Devices. The class of computer hardware that includes terminals and data entry devices is concerned primarily with communication between a person and a computer or another form of computer equipment. As mentioned previously, the choice of terminals is important because they tend to have a long-term effect on the total system. The computer may be transparent to the terminal operator, but the terminal is not; moreover, terminals are replaced less frequently than computers. Equipment in this classification can be grouped into four categories: batch, interactive, and intelligent terminals, and data entry devices.

Communication between a person and a computer

A *batch terminal,* which is used for remote job entry and remote job output, consists of an assembly of input/output devices and mass-storage units. A modern batch terminal is likely to include a minicomputer for control, and typical comments are a video display, card reader, and line printer.

Batch terminal

An *interactive terminal* is typically used for such applications as time sharing, text editing, problem solving, on-line banking, reservations, and message composition. Interactive terminals are classed as keyboard/printer or video, and they characteristically consist of a keyboard and character-by-character printer or a keyboard and CRT (cathode-ray tube) display, respectively.

Interactive terminal

An *intelligent terminal* has a built-in microcomputer, normally used for prompting the operator and verifying data input. Intelligent terminals consist of a microprocessor, a read-only memory, a random-access memory, and sometimes a storage unit, such as cassette or floppy disk, in addition to a keyboard and output facility. The microcomputer can also perform logging, formatting, code conversion, and file maintenance; typical applications include data entry, POS service,* transaction processing, graphics, and local data processing.

Intelligent terminal

Data entry devices are the class of equipment whereby an operator participates in the process of putting data into machine-readable form. The process, which can be performed with an interactive or an intelligent terminal, traditionally includes the use of punched cards, punched tape, special optical readers, and also badge readers. However, as a separate class of device, data entry devices normally consist of a keyboard, video display, and a connection to a magnetic disk or tape unit. The process may include the use of a minicomputer and is associated with the terms *keytape* and *keydisk.*

Data entry devices

---

* POS is an acronym for *point of sale* or *point of service* and refers to the "cash register" or "financial terminal" class of devices.

SYSTEMS SOFTWARE

Software: set of computer programs

Systems software is a general name for the set of computer programs that effectively manages the hardware and information resources of an information system and serves as the interface between applications-related programs and the physical hardware units of the computer system. Also included are programs that facilitate the preparation of user-written programs. Systems software is usually, but not always, provided by the computer manufacturer. In some instances, systems software developed by one vendor is used in computer installations supplied by other vendors—this is sometimes the case with IBM replaceable central processing units. Systems software is divided into four categories:

Compilers, translators, generators, and interpreters
Operating systems
Data management systems
Data communications systems

In modern computer systems, there is a close relationship between hardware and systems software. In fact, each is indispensable to the other in satisfying system-design objectives.

Programs that process programs

Language Processors. Compilers, translators, generators, and interpreters, commonly referred to as *language processors,* serve to translate a user-prepared program to machine-executable form or, in the case of an interpreter, to interpretively execute a program. The widespread use of standardized languages for program development increases the portability of software and facilitates the programming process.

Control, executive, or monitor programs

Operating Systems. Operating systems software, also known as the "control program," is concerned with controlling the operation of the total computer hardware system and managing its hardware resources. Through the use of an effective operating system, a computer installation can increase the efficiency of computer operations. In the modern era of computers, most small installations and virtually all medium- and large-sized installations use the services of an operating system.

Data Management. Data management is involved with the manner in which data are stored and accessed from peripheral (and mass-storage) devices external to the computer's central processing and main storage units. Data management facilities are normally incorporated into the total operating system environment.

Input/output and storage management programs

Data Communications. Data communications systems software is concerned with communications-oriented tasks, such as line control, error checking, code conversion, addressing, polling, and message assembly and disassembly. In brief, data communications software permits an information systems designer to specify complete control over network components and, at the same time, provide device independence to application programs.

Network architecture and control programs

APPLICATION SUBSYSTEMS

Application subsystems is a class of computer software that serves as an interface between a user and the computer or between an application program and the systems software. An application subsystem is usually developed by a computer vendor or a software house and exists as a large set of complex programs that perform relatively sophisticated functions. Examples of applications subsystems are:

Sophisticated applications software

Data base management system is a collection of programs, concepts, and operational procedures that permits data to be centralized and stored for use in one or more applications. In a data base, redundant data are factored out and duplicate details integrated, resulting in increased data processing capability and a decreased need for multiple file updates. A data base is normally accessed through an application program, which references the data base management system (DBMS). The DBMS then accesses the data files through the data management system.

Data base

Reservation system is a special application subsystem that permits a user at a terminal to access an integrated set of specially prepared files. Typical examples are airline and hotel reservation systems. The reservation system uses the facilities of the operating system, data management system, and the data communications system to perform respective processing functions.

Reservations

Remote access

On-line system is a subsystem that permits a user at a remote location to access the computer to enter or retrieve information. This facility is more general than a reservation system. Normally, the on-line system invokes specially written programs, such as for marketing, finance, and manufacturing, which permit the user to access the computer in a characteristic fashion. On-line systems also use the functions provided by the systems software.

Physical control

Process control system allows the computer to be connected to a physical apparatus for purposes of control or data collection. The practice of doing this type of application is complicated, and the subsystem serves to keep the level of detail low enough to enable application programs to be written to generate or analyze data.

Clearly, the use of application subsystems affects more people than does traditional systems software. This is the layered effect achieved through the "building block" approach to computer utilization. Overall, the process of using application subsystems is cost-effective, as compared to total in-house development of software, and results in a more reliable operating environment.

APPLICATION PROGRAMS

Day-to-day computing

Application programs is a class of computer software that relates to the day-to-day computing of an organization. Traditional applications in this category involve data processing, problem-solving, modeling and simulation, data analysis, and so forth. Application programs may be purchased from a software vendor or developed in-house. In either case, the programs may be used for a long period of time or used a few times and then discarded. Programs that are used for an extended period normally go through a life cycle, involving development, testing, implementation (i.e., the process of putting the programs to actual use), and finally cessation.

EVOLUTION OF COMPUTERS AND DATA PROCESSING

The use of computer technology has evolved from manually operated unit record systems, known as "tabulating machines," to automatically operated large-scale computer systems with on-line processing capability. The process of evolution is enlightening because it provides a snapshot of information technology at various stages of development.

In the era of unit record systems the primary input and storage medium was punched cards. Machine-generated output was punched cards and the printed page. A separate machine existed for each step in the processing cycle (e.g., sorting and printing), and punched cards were manually transported from one machine to the next. The functions of the various unit record machines were controlled by a wired control panel, and each machine was manually operated.

Start of punched-card era

With the advent of card-oriented computers, the previously distinct processing steps were integrated into a computer program. Even though manual operations still prevailed, the total amount of manual intervention was considerably less because one machine was employed to do the complete job. At this point, two modes of computer operation prevailed: closed shop and open shop. With the *closed shop* mode, only designated computer operators could operate the computer. With the *open shop* mode, any qualified user could operate the computer.

Early computers

Closed v. open shop

Advances in storage media, which included magnetic tape and magnetic disk, paved the way for advanced methods of computer utilization. The first major advance involved the use of an operating system to provide job-to-job transition and to manage the resources of the computer system. In addition, the efficiency of computer utilization increases through multiprogramming techniques, whereby more than one job resides in the computer and the multiprogramming system switches control to another job when idle time is encountered in the current job. Finally, time-sharing systems, with which a user could interact with the computer via telecommunications facilities to enter or run a program, completed the transition in technology from manual systems to readily accessible computational facilities.

Advanced methods of computer use

Recent advances in information technology have been achieved through organization, in contradistinction to advances made solely by way of technical innovation. Characteristic systems in this category are: computer networks, distributed systems, and distributed data base systems. A *computer network* is a collection of computers and terminals connected by a communications system. This classification necessarily includes a variety of time-sharing or on-line systems. In its most general sense, the classification refers to a network in which two or more computer complexes are

Information dynamics: processing + communications + data

connected via a communications system. In a *distributed system,* the processing is parceled out among regional processing centers that comprise a computer network. Information flows within the network according to organizational work patterns. The most recent major advance is the *distributed data base* in which a data base is partitioned among regional processing centers connected as a computer network.

Data processing evolution

Clearly, the evolution of information technology embodies the processes of innovation of new technology and of principles of organization. At first, new technology replaces old technology to achieve the first level in an evolutionary step, and second, the system is reorganized to achieve the second level of advancement. The two-step process then continues accordingly.

USERS AND SUBJECTS

Computer interaction

The class of computers and the scope of people affected by information have changed dramatically as the computer field has evolved. Today, the average person interacts with the computer in one way or another at least once a day. With the acceptance of electronic funds-transfer systems, the frequency is expected to increase. Excluding the "person on the street," the people involved with information technology in everyday business or professional activity can be classed as follows:

Computer users

Programmers
Systems analysts
Data entry personnel
Managers
Administrators
Clerical personnel
Technical personnel
Professionals

The range of people affected extends from clerks in a warehouse to physicians and attorneys. The level of skill required obviously depends on the hardware/software systems used and where they fall in the total operating environment.

The preceding group is relatively small compared with the total number of people about whom information is stored. Information about most if not all of us is stored in a multiplicity of information systems maintained by both public and private organizations. The scope of these information systems extends far beyond the file cabinets and dossiers with which we are familiar. Information systems can and do affect our daily lives, and only through an understanding of information technology can we properly assess its overall impact.

Data subjects

SUMMARY

Information technology is informally defined as the use of computer hardware, software, data communications technology, and information that have been integrated in a systems environment in such a manner as to have a synergistic effect on the performance of the various components. Information technology is a dynamic subject, and thus its relationship to the organization and to individuals in the organization must constantly be monitored. The need for informational resources in modern society is very great; however, the unquestioned acceptance of modern technology may result in undesirable side effects.

An information system is an organized collection of computer hardware components, computer software, application programs, data, and organizational procedures that is specifically configured and managed to support the operations, decisionmaking, and planning functions of an organization. One means of viewing the relationship among the various components of an information system is to employ the "onionskin" approach, wherein technology is synthesized and used in a layered fashion. Proceeding outward from the core of an information system, one can uncover the following elements:

Computer system components *(core)*
Systems software
Application subsystems
Application programs
Users *(outer layer)*

An information system supports organizational functions in the general form of an information pyramid. Organizational functions at the top of the pyramid deal with policy matters and require a lesser amount of detailed information than do organizational functions at the bottom of the pyramid. Accordingly, policy matters directly or indirectly affect a larger segment of the organization than do operational matters, which primarily affect the group involved.

More specifically, computer system components include computers, peripheral devices, data communications equipment, terminals, and data entry devices. Each of these categories is further subdivided according to functions that the components perform. *Systems software* is a general name for the set of computer programs that manages the hardware and information resources of an information system and serves as the interface between applications-related programs and the physical hardware units of the computer system. Systems software includes language processors, operating systems, data management systems, and data communications systems.

Application subsystems is a class of computer software that serves as an interface between a user and the computer or between an application program and the systems software. Normally classed as applications subsystems are data base management systems, reservation systems, on-line systems, and process control systems. Application programs relate to the day-to-day computing of an organization and incorporate the traditional areas of data processing, problem-solving, modeling, simulation, and data analysis.

The use of computer technology has evolved from manually operated unit-record systems to automatically operated large-scale computer systems with on-line processing capability. Systems have also evolved that affect a larger class of both computer users and data subjects.

IMPORTANT TERMS AND CONCEPTS

The reader should be familiar with the following terms and concepts:

Application programs
Application subsystems
Batch terminal
Card reader
Central processing unit
Closed shop
Computer
Computer network
Computer system components

Data communications equipment
Data base management system
Data communications channel
Data communications system
Data management system
Disk storage unit
Distributed data base
Distributed system
Information pyramid
Information system
Information technology
Intelligent terminal
Interactive terminal
Language processor
Large-scale computer
Line printer
Magnetic tape unit
Main storage unit
Medium-scale computer
Microcomputer
Minicomputer
Network equipment
Network processor
Onionskin approach
On-line system
Open shop
Operating system
Peripheral device
Process control system
Reservation system
Systems software
Terminal
Users

READINGS AND REFERENCES

Blanc, R. P. and I. W. Cotton. *Computer Networking*. New York: IEEE Press, 1976.

Cougar, J. D. and F. R. McFadden. *Introduction to Computer-Based Information Systems*. New York: John Wiley & Sons, 1975.

Katzan, H. *An Introduction to Distributed Data Processing*. Princeton: Petrocelli Books, 1979.

————. *Introduction to Computers and Data Processing*. New York: D. Van Nostrand Company, 1979.

Li, D. H. *Design and Management of Information Systems*. Chicago: Science Research Associates, 1972.

Lucas, H. C., Jr. *Information Systems Concepts for Management*. New York: McGraw-Hill Book Company, 1978.

Privacy Protection Study Commission. *Technology and Privacy*. Report of the Privacy Protection Study Commission, Appendix 5. Washington, D.C.: U.S. Government Printing Office, Stock No. 057–003–00425–9, 1977.

Simon, H. A. *Administrative Behavior: A Study of Decision-Making Processes in Administrative Organization*. New York: Macmillan, 1957.

4
PERSONAL PRIVACY IN RECORDKEEPING SYSTEMS

The present concern over privacy arises from the interplay between modern recordkeeping technology, made possible largely by computer-based systems and telecommunications, and the needs of society for information—needed to function efficiently, or even at all, and to comply with various government legislative regulations.

WILLIS H. WARE

One of the toughest problems facing the computer industry is data protection. The problem is multifaceted, involving physical facilities, operational procedures, computer hardware features, and programming and software conventions. In addition, data protection is related to the broader social issue of privacy, which frequently becomes an emotional topic. The situation is summarized very well by Arthur R. Miller:[1]

Privacy and data protection

> The new information technologies seem to have given birth to a new social virus—"data-mania." Its symptoms are shortness of breath and heart palpitations when contemplating a new computer application, a feeling of possessiveness about information and a deep resentment toward those who won't yield it, a delusion that all information handlers can walk on water, and a highly advanced case of astigmatism that prevents the affected victim from perceiving anything but the intrinsic value of data. Fortunately, only some members of the information-handling fraternity have been stricken by the disease.

[1] Miller, A. R. *The Assault on Privacy: Computers, Data Banks, and Dossiers.* p. 37. Ann Arbor, Michigan: The University of Michigan Press, 1971.

Informational needs are important to government and the private community

We live in an information-based society that exhibits a growing propensity for collecting and storing information. Although information gathering is usually associated with such governmental agencies as the Census Bureau, the U.S. Department of Defense, the Office of Economic Opportunity, and various loyalty-security groups, informational needs and associated precautions are equally important to the private community and are in widespread use. In short, the effective use of information enables an organization to improve the efficiency of its operation.

Computers and data protection

Organizations have always collected information of various kinds. However, in recent years, problems have become apparent due to the widespread use of computers, information systems, and telecommunications facilities. Computers have not created a data protection problem or even the privacy problem; the effective use of computers, however, has enlarged the scope of information gathering. Thus, greater and greater quantities of information can be collected, recorded, and later retrieved at a moment's notice. Therein lies the problem. In earlier times, physical barriers such as walls and file cabinets offered some degree of security to decentralized files. In many cases, the value of information was simply not worth the effort required to obtain it. In modern computer-based information systems, however, access to information is frequently more convenient and more efficient—regardless of whether the intrusion is planned or unplanned and independent of the nature of the information being accessed.

PRIVACY

The subject of privacy is a controversial and emotional topic. This book is not primarily concerned with privacy, yet the topic provides much of the "motivation" for effective data regulation.

Privacy provides a partial motivation for data regulation

Data protection is given the most attention when the privacy of an individual or an organization is jeopardized. According to Alan F. Westin:[2]

> Privacy is the claim of individuals, groups, or institutions to determine for themselves when, how, and to what extent information about them is communicated to others.

[2] Westin, A. F. *Privacy and Freedom,* p. 7. New York: Atheneum, 1967. Courtesy of Atheneum, New York, and of the Bodley Head, London.

Privacy is significantly related to data protection because it is an integral part of society and affects the behavior of its members. Much of the non-computer-based literature on privacy is concerned with the physical state of being private. Westin defines four states of individual privacy: solitude, intimacy, anonymity, and reserve. *Solitude* implies physical separation from the group; *intimacy* implies participation in a small unit that achieves corporate solitude; *anonymity* implies freedom from identification and surveillance while in a public environment; and *reserve* implies the creation of a psychological barrier that protects the individual from unwanted intrusion.[3]

Physical states of being private

These states serve one or more functions for the individual. Privacy is frequently used to attain *personal autonomy,* wherein hopes, fears, shame, and aspirations are hidden. Privacy is also used to obtain *emotional release* and to carry on *self-evaluation.* From the standpoint of data protection, the most significant function served by privacy is that of *limited and protected communication,* which protects the individual against the disclosure of confidential information to unauthorized persons or groups. An example of such communication is the legal privilege of confidentiality in their professional relationships that is granted to doctors, lawyers, and the clergy. *The normal functions served by privacy, as just outlined, should also be an integral part of an effective data protection program.*

Reasons for privacy

Concerns for privacy should be an integral part of a data protection program

An organization requires privacy to achieve its basic objectives. Government agencies, private businesses, political parties, and fraternal groups—to name only a few—all need freedom from exposure of competitive products, decision-making processes, internal operational procedures, and damaging information about organization members. In many cases, the effectiveness of an organization is based on its "image" or "outward appearance," so that the disclosure of its private internal affairs would be detrimental to its success. In others, timing and private communications spell the difference between success and failure.

Privacy is needed to realize basic organizational objectives

Westin also points out another aspect of privacy, which has important implications for data protection: the seemingly universal tendency of individuals to invade the privacy of others and of society to engage in surveillance to enforce its norms.[4] At the individual level, curiosity, gossip, the

There is a universal tendency for individuals and society to invade the privacy of others

[3] Westin, op. cit., p. 31.
[4] Westin, op. cit., p. 19.

Although personal surveillance is socially approved, the individual does not have control over his or her informational profile

search for explanations, and even the desire for vicarious experience exist in all societies and at different levels of society. At the societal level, socially approved methods of surveillance are used by authoritative agencies to protect the rules and customs of a society. Even though personal surveillance is generally governed by law, the individual usually has neither control over the accuracy of his or her informational profile[5] nor knowledge of the agencies between which the information is transferred. Information transfer becomes a data protection problem when the receiving party does not have the authority to receive (or to collect) it. Unsanctioned access to information by an agency employee and the use of that information for personal gain or for transfer to persons of another agency are other potential but very real problems.

Clearly, legal and moral issues have been raised that are beyond the scope of data protection in computer-based information systems and in associated data regulation practices. Even though secure computer systems per se cannot control the behavior of individuals desiring to obtain personal information, legal sanctions can guarantee autonomy of choice in certain private areas, so that persons would have less to fear even if information about them were more widely accessible. Therefore, the combination of technical advances in data security and legal sanctions to guarantee freedom of choice would constitute a "double-barreled" approach to the data protection and data regulation situation.

Legal sanctions can guarantee autonomy of choice

INFORMATIONAL CONTROL

Privacy safeguards are needed to prevent the exercise of power through information

Due to the widespread application of computer and communications technology, there has been a gradual trend among private institutions and government agencies to ignore the individual's need for privacy. Privacy safeguards are the individual's sole line of defense against the exercise of power through information control. Individuals can lose control of information about themselves in three ways:

1. Information obtained against the subject's wishes.
2. Information obtained from an agency against the wishes of the agency and of the subject.

[5] Miller, op. cit., p. 47.

3. Information willingly disclosed by the beneficial user or agency but against the subject's wishes.

In the case of *information obtained against a subject's wishes,* an area in which privacy is normally expected is invaded. This category includes explicit attempts to obtain information and implicit methods wherein a subject is forced to disclose personal information. Some typical actions are:

Information obtained against a subject's wishes

1. *Searches and seizure:* includes assault or trespass without special authorization (such as a warrant).
2. *Electronic surveillance:* includes wiretapping and bugging.
3. *Compelled self-disclosure:* includes threat of criminal punishment, general governmental reporting requirements (such as tax information), and governmental registration and recordkeeping (such as selective service registration and the census).
4. *Informers and secret agents:* includes obtaining information through agents and informers that infiltrate certain groups, from individuals that masquerade as public officials to obtain private information from citizens, and through other forms of disguise and trickery.
5. *Participant monitoring with electronic devices:* includes recording conversations without the knowledge of the subjects, thereby eliminating the protection of limited dissemination. (This category also includes supervisory monitoring, of which neither party is aware.)
6. *Observation of public occurrences and permanent recording of transient information:* includes regulation by surveillance and the piecing together of intelligence data to create "new" information.
7. *Consent to giving private information:* includes cases where the subject is coerced into giving private information, for fear of reprisal of some sort. (Typical cases include employer and government requests for "voluntary" information.)
8. *Disclosure as a condition for a privilege, enjoyment of a benefit, or avoidance of harm:* includes disclosures a person would prefer not to make but that are necessary to obtain a desired benefit (such as a driver's license or charge account) or to avoid an undesired consequence (such as a lie-detector test to avoid dismissal from a job).

Personal intrusion may be direct or indirect

Dividing line between willing disclosure and unauthorized access is obscure

The dividing line between willing and unauthorized disclosure is obscure because some benefit is frequently associated with disclosure. Therefore, even though individuals may consent to a disclosure of information, they may still feel that their privacy has been invaded.

Information obtained from an agency against the wishes of the agency or subject

Agency is responsible for providing adequate data protection

Technical advances in data protection are often offset by cost

In the case of *information obtained from an agency against the wishes of the agency and of the subject,* the same requirements for the protection of information should apply to the agency as apply to the subject. The client confidentiality privilege of the medical and legal professions is an example. This case is normally of concern in two situations:

1. *Security of computer systems.* It is the agency's responsibility to provide a satisfactory level of data protection; however, technological advances in data protection are frequently offset by the agency's desire to minimize costs. Effective countermeasures are (1) to collect and store information only when it is absolutely needed and (2) to destroy information when it is no longer needed. There is a tendency in computer-based information systems to retain information because the cost of doing so is relatively inexpensive.

Information in recordkeeping systems is often retained because it is inexpensive to do so

2. *Unauthorized access and use of private information by persons with normal access to that information.* Security against unauthorized insiders can be countered through a "need to know" restriction that is enforced by the agency.

Information disclosed by the agency or beneficial user against the subject's wishes

In the case of *information willingly disclosed by the beneficial user or agency but against the subject's wishes,* information is normally disclosed to a wider audience than the subject expected. Informers, interagency transfers, and information trade-offs (such as between police and reporter) fall into this category. In addition, accuracy is of concern here because information may be inaccurately recorded, out of date, or disseminated for purposes other than those for which it was originally recorded. In the private sector, this area is commonly associated with the collection, dissemination, accuracy, and relevance of third-party information regarding credit profiles.

Accuracy of information

The notion that "information is power" has particular relevance for computer-based recordkeeping systems, whether they exist in the public or private sector. Some of the most obvious considerations are:

1. Information not collected does not have to be protected.
2. Unneeded information should be destroyed.
3. Inaccurate information should be corrected or destroyed.
4. The level of danger of disclosure of information is related to the amount of private information that persons supply to recordkeepers.
5. Some restrictions should exist on the kinds of information that certain organizations should possess.

Safeguards against "information is power"

Clearly, the use of computers has not created the privacy problem. However, their use does increase the availability of information and permits, in some cases, the personalization of data originally collected as "nonpersonal" in nature. A typical case here is census data that allow neighborhood breakdowns.

Computers only compound the problem

Another possible threat to privacy involves the cashless society into which we are moving. In electronic funds transfer (EFT), an audit trail of the nature and amount of individual transactions is created. An "information profile" created by piecing together otherwise unrelated data can be as much a violation of privacy as can an explicit act of intrusion.

Electronic funds transfer and the "information profile"

RECORDKEEPING

Since the Stone Age, recordkeeping has been an important function of society. Historically, three types of records have been kept about people: administrative, intelligence, and statistical.

Societal recordkeeping

Administrative records are maintained by government agencies and private organizations. An administrative record normally contains identifying information, such as a name or social security number, and is generated by an everyday transaction, such as obtaining a driver's license or a marriage license, or making a business credit arrangement. Personal data in an administrative record are supplied by the subject or can be readily observed from normal activities. Government administrative records are usually open to inspection, whereas the administrative records of most private firms are proprietary. Some administrative records serve as a person's credentials—for example, birth certificate, diploma, military discharge papers, and immigration papers.

Administrative records: data are normally supplied by subject

Intelligence records: information is gathered

Intelligence records are usually but not always maintained by government agencies. Typical intelligence records may involve a security clearance, a police investigation, or a credit report. Intelligence records, which are seldom made public, circulate among intelligence-gathering organizations.

Statistical records: data are synthesized

Statistical records are normally synthesized through a questionnaire or its equivalent, such as a population census or a sample survey. In almost all cases, identifying data for a subject are not stored with the statistical data, and thus a certain amount of anonymity is inherent in this kind of record-keeping. Although data from administrative records can be used for statistical purposes, statistical records are generally not used for administrative or intelligence purposes.

In modern computer-based information systems, record-keeping activities cannot be neatly placed in any of the three categories just given. Nevertheless, three traditions exist with regard to government records about people:

Traditional practices in recordkeeping systems

- An organization should record only information that has a clear-cut relevance to its concerns. Religious data, for example, should not be recorded where there is no state-supported church, and citizens should not be required to furnish extraneous data as the price of obtaining a benefit.
- As much as possible, information that has been collected should be held in public files so that public scrutiny can act as a check on the arbitrary exercise of administrative authority. Closed files in government should be the exception, and their content and use should be regulated by specific laws, both to limit their extent and to assure their confidentiality.
- The three types of records described above should be held separately, and each should be used only for its nominal purpose. The transfer of data from one type of record to another should take place only under controlled conditions. Records that do not fall neatly into one category, and record systems whose structure or use blurs the boundaries between types of records, demand special safeguards to protect personal privacy.[6]

These traditions are reflected in a recommended Code of Fair Information Practice, which lists five principles concerning safeguards for automated personal data systems:

[6] U.S. Dept. of Health, Education, and Welfare. *Records, Computers, and the Rights of Citizens.* Report of the Secretary's Advisory Committee on Automated Personal Data Systems, p. 6–7. Cambridge, Massachusetts: The M.I.T. Press, 1973. Courtesy of M.I.T. Press.

- There must be no personal data record-keeping systems whose very existence is secret.
- There must be a way for an individual to find out what information about him is in a record and how it is used.
- There must be a way for an individual to prevent information about him that was obtained for one purpose from being used or made available for other purposes without his consent.
- There must be a way for an individual to correct or amend a record of identifiable information about him.
- Any organization creating, maintaining, using, or disseminating records of identifiable personal data must assure the reliability of the data for their intended use and must take precautions to prevent misuse of the data.[7]

Principles of Fair Information Practice

These traditions and principles are formalized in Appendix A, Safeguard Requirements for Administrative Personal Data Systems, and in Appendix B, Safeguard Requirements for Statistical Reporting and Research Systems. The traditions, principles, and requirements have been implemented as data regulations, in whole or in part, in several countries.

THE PRIVACY ACT OF 1974: A CASE STUDY

The various reasons for the Privacy Act of 1974, are listed as follows:

The Congress finds that—
(1) the privacy of an individual is directly affected by the collection, maintenance, use, and dissemination of personal information by Federal agencies;
(2) the increasing use of computers and sophisticated information technology, while essential to the efficient operations of the Government, has greatly magnified the harm to individual privacy that can occur from any collection, maintenance, use, or dissemination of personal information;
(3) the opportunities for an individual to secure employment, insurance, and credit, and his right to due process, and other legal protections are endangered by the misuse of certain information systems;
(4) the right to privacy is a personal and fundamental right protected by the Constitution of the United States; and
(5) in order to protect the privacy of individuals identified in information systems maintained by Federal agencies, it is

Reasons for the Privacy Act of 1974

[7] Ibid, p. xx–xxi.

necessary and proper for the Congress to regulate the collection, maintenance, use, and dissemination of information by such agencies."[8]

The purposes of the Privacy Act of 1974 are:

. . .to provide certain safeguards for an individual against an invasion of personal privacy by requiring Federal agencies, except as otherwise provided by law, to—

Congressional objectives

(1) permit an individual to determine what records pertaining to him are collected, maintained, used, or disseminated by such agencies;

(2) permit an individual to prevent records pertaining to him obtained by such agencies for a particular purpose from being used or made available for another purpose without his consent;

(3) permit an individual to gain access to information pertaining to him in Federal agency records, to have a copy made of all or any portion thereof, and to correct or amend such records;

(4) collect, maintain, use, or disseminate any record of identifiable personal information in a manner that assures that such action is for a necessary and lawful purpose, that the information is current and accurate for its intended use, and that adequate safeguards are provided to prevent misuse of such information;

(5) permit exemptions from the requirements with respect to records provided in this Act only in those cases where there is an important public policy need for such exemption as has been determined by specific statutory authority; and

(6) be subject to civil suit for any damages which occur as a result of willful or intentional action which violates any individual's rights under this Act.[9]

Procedural requirements

The act includes a variety of procedural requirements for federal agencies, ranging from annual reporting in the *Federal Register* to the administration of the provisions of the act. Possibly the most far-reaching aspects of the act relate to the five principles concerning safeguards for automated personal data systems (see p. 48). In the Privacy Act of 1974, Congress implicitly expanded these principles:

(1) There shall be no personal-data record-keeping system whose very existence is secret and there shall be a policy of

---

[8] Public Law 93–579, The Privacy Act of 1974, sec. 2(a).
[9] Ibid, sec. 2(b).

openness about an organization's personal-data record-keeping policies, practices, and systems. (The Openness Principle)

(2) An individual about whom information is maintained by a record-keeping organization in individually identifiable form shall have a right to see and copy that information. (The Individual Access Principle)

(3) An individual about whom information is maintained by a record-keeping organization shall have a right to correct or amend the substance of that information. (The Individual Participation Principle)

(4) There shall be limits on the types of information an organization may collect about an individual, as well as certain requirements with respect to the manner in which it collects such information. (The Collection Limitation Principle)

(5) There shall be limits on the internal uses of information about an individual within a record-keeping organization. (The Use Limitation Principle)

(6) There shall be limits on the external disclosures of information about an individual a record-keeping organization may make. (The Disclosure Limitation Principle)

(7) A record-keeping organization shall bear an affirmative responsibility for establishing reasonable and proper information management policies and practices which assure that its collection, maintenance, use, and dissemination of information about an individual is necessary and lawful and the information itself is current and accurate. (The Information Management Principle)

(8) A record-keeping organization shall be accountable for its personal-data record-keeping policies, practices, and systems. (The Accountability Principle)[10]

Each of the eight principles is discussed separately in the Privacy Act of 1974, the text of which is contained in Appendix C.

The *Openness Principle* facilitates public scrutiny of federal agency recordkeeping activities and enables interested citizens to be aware of systems in which personal records are likely to exist. This principle establishes that no agency may conceal the existence of any personal-data recordkeeping system. To accomplish that end, system notices are published in the *Federal Register*. Moreover, the Privacy Act Statement

Openness

[10] Privacy Protection Study Commission. *The Privacy Act of 1974: An Assessment.* Report of the Privacy Protection Study Commission, Appendix 4, pp. 76–77. Washington, D.C.: U.S. Government Printing Office, Stock No. 052–003–0042401. 1977.

specifies the authority for data collection, given at the time that information is solicited from individuals.

Individual access

The *Individual Access Principle* permits individuals to see and copy records that an agency maintains about them, without resorting to other administrative means, such as the Freedom of Information Act (FOIA). This principle generally clarifies previously existing uncertainties regarding an individual's right to see and copy personal records concerning existing Freedom of Information Act exemptions and refusals for information disclosure based on a ''deliberative processes of government'' clause, which are occasionally encountered.

Individual participation

The *Individual Participation Principle* provides the individual with the right to challenge the contents of a record on the grounds that it is not accurate, timely, complete, or relevant. Thus, the individual has some degree of control over personal information collected or revealed.

Collection limitation

The *Collection Limitation Principle* places reasonable limits on what information is collected, and how. Thus, agencies may only collect information that is relevant and necessary to a lawful purpose. Also, this information must be collected directly from the subject, where practical. An agency must also give a Privacy Act Statement and not use the social security number as an identifier.

Use limitation

The *Use Limitation Principle* governs the manner in which information about an individual can be used. In general, information collected by an agency can only be disclosed to officers of that agency and to employees who need that information to perform their duties. A subject can determine the internal use of information through the Privacy Act Statement. One drawback of the statement, however, is that future uses of information, outside the control of the agency, cannot be anticipated.

Disclosure limitation

The *Disclosure Limitation Principle* concerns the external disclosure of information by an agency. The Privacy Act authorizes ten categories of disclosure that may be made without the subject's consent. Included is the ''routine-use'' case, which refers to the disclosure of information for a purpose compatible with that for which it was collected. The routine-use case is widely used among law-enforcement agencies to facilitate the flow of information.

Information management

The *Information Management Principle* concerns the manner in which information is managed. It recognizes a set of norms relating to policies and procedures that should be established and maintained. Some degree of accountability for effective information management is placed on the agency so that the subjects do not have the full responsibility of monitoring records about themselves. This principle also governs the necessity for, and the timeliness, completeness, and relevancy of, information stored about a subject. Finally, it requires an agency to maintain a record of disclosures of information about a subject, to propagate corrections, and to conduct internal auditing and Privacy Act compliance monitoring.

Timeliness, completeness, and relevancy of information

The *Accountability Principle* determines that a federal agency can be held accountable for its personal-data recordkeeping policies and procedures, and in particular, for adherence to the seven previous principles. This accountability is exercised through an individual's rights to:

Accountability principle

1. See, copy, and challenge the contents of personal records about himself or herself.
2. Review an agency's accounting of disclosures of such personal records.
3. Sue for any damages incurred thereby.

Individual's rights

In general, enforcement is important since it is difficult to establish willful or intentional behavior on the part of the agency, and government contractors and grantees are not directly liable under the Privacy Act for violations.

Practical limitations exist to the effectiveness of legislation concerned with human values and individual liberties, such as the Privacy Act of 1974. The situation is summarized well by the Privacy Protection Study Commission:

> There are some important information policy issues the Act either ignores or does not address adequately. For example, in almost any discussion of the intent of the Privacy Act, mention is made of limiting the amount of information agencies actually collect about individuals. There is a commonly held belief, evident in the Act's legislative history and voiced by numerous agency personnel, that the Act was intended to reduce the amount of information the Federal government collects about individuals. Yet the fact of the matter is that the Act only establishes the outer boundaries of legitimate government inquiry, and it does so in a way that reflects rather closely the boundaries that had grown up prior to the Act's passage. Similarly, as the discus-

Practical limitations

ion of the routine-use provision indicated, transfers of information among agencies have only been slightly reduced as a result of the Act's passage.[11]

Data protection is a complex issue

Clearly, the protection of personal data systems turned out to be a more complex issue than most people anticipated. As mentioned in the Privacy Protection Study Commission Report, the problem is not premeditated intrusion into personal privacy but is inherent in the government's growing use of computer and communications technology. This conclusion is summarized in the report:

> The real danger is the gradual erosion of individual liberties through the automation, integration, and interconnection of many small, separate record-keeping systems, each of which alone may seem innocuous, even benevolent, and wholly justifiable.[12]

APPLICATIONS: TAX AND EMPLOYMENT RECORDS

Tax and employment records contain self-disclosed personal information

Two recordkeeping activities that relate to the day-to-day life of most individuals involve tax and employment records. In both cases, the records contain a substantial amount of personal information that an individual would probably not otherwise disclose. Moreover, the disclosure of tax and employment information cannot be considered voluntary, since the former is required by tax law and the latter is usually required in order to obtain and sustain continued employment.

The protection of personal tax information applies to local, state, and federal jurisdictions—even though the consideration of disclosure policies is normally associated with the Internal Revenue Service (IRS). In considering the relationship between the citizen and the IRS, the Privacy Protection Study Commision stated:

Individual v. IRS

> The disclosure to other government agencies of information about individual taxpayers has increased steadily since 1910. In most instances, new uses of such information were authorized administratively and without any real opportunity for public debate.[13]

---

[11] Ibid, p. 107.
[12] Ibid, p. 108.
[13] Privacy Protection Study Commission. *The Citizen as Taxpayer*. Report of the Privacy Protection Study Commission, Appendix 2, p. 27. Washington, D.C: U.S. Government Printing Office, Stock No. 052–003–00422–4, 1977.

In developing its recommendations regarding the disclosure of tax information, the Privacy Protection Study commission recognized that the individual is at a disadvantage with regard to the IRS. The IRS can compel the disclosure of information under threat of punishment. In addition, the United States tax system is based on the cooperation of the taxpayers and the confidentiality of tax returns. These conditions dictate that dissemination of tax information be tightly controlled, even though other agencies may have pressing demands for information without the authority to collect it. This form of analysis led to the formulation of four general recommendations by the commission regarding IRS tax disclosure:

Conditions dictate tight control over information

(1) that no disclosure of individually identifiable data by the Internal Revenue Service be permitted unless the individual to whom the information pertains has consented to such disclosure in writing or unless the disclosure is specifically authorized by Federal statute;

Recommendations concerning IRS tax disclosure

(2) that the Congress itself specify by statute the categories of tax information the IRS can disclose and the purposes for which the information can be used, rather than delegate general discretionary authority in this matter to the Commissioner of Internal Revenue or any other representative of the Executive Branch;
(3) that the IRS be prohibited from disclosing any more individually identifiable taxpayer information than is necessary to accomplish the purpose for which the disclosure has been authorized, and that the IRS adopt administrative procedures to facilitate public scrutiny of its compliance with this requirement; and
(4) that recipients of tax information from the Internal Revenue Service be prohibited from redisclosing it without the written consent of the taxpayer, unless the redisclosure is specifically authorized by Federal statute.[14]

The Privacy Protection Study Commission then states that the recommendations were effectively embodied in the Tax Reform Act of 1976. (Prior to 1976, tax returns were regarded as public records.) The general rule, now established by Section 6103(a) of the Internal Revenue Code, is that "returns and return information shall be confidential.[15]

Tax Reform Act of 1976

Historically, the growth in employee recordkeeping has

---

[14] Ibid, p. 29.
[15] Ibid p. 30.

Employment records: individual v. organization

paralleled the growth of modern work organizations. Today's large organization is typically characterized by a high degree of specialization and a well-defined set of standardized policies and procedures for managing day-to-day operations. Thus, it follows that personnel management would stress rational decisionmaking with regard to the selection, assignment, and promotion of personnel. This concern can be translated into a set of personnel objectives:

1. Equal treatment for all employees.
2. Relying on expertise, skills, and experience relevant to the position.

Personnel objectives

3. No extraorganizational prerogatives of the position, that is, the position belongs to the organization, not to the person.
4. Introducing specific standards of work and output.
5. Keeping complete records and files.
6. Setting up and enforcing rules and regulations that serve the interests of the organization.
7. Recognizing that the rules and regulations are binding upon managers as well as employees.[16]

These objectives are related to privacy protection through records created before and after hiring. *Records created before hiring normally include:*[17]

Before hiring

Application forms
Background checks
References
Interviewer evaluations
Medical records
Tests

Records created after hiring normally include:[18]

After hiring

Demographic data
Basic payroll data and employment information
Time, attendance, and classification information
Personal information
Verification documents

[16] Privacy Protection Study Commission. *Employment Records.* Report of the Privacy Protection Study Commission, Appendix 3, pp. 3–4. Washington, D.C.: U.S. Government Printing Office, Stock No. 052–003–00423–2, 1977.
[17] Ibid, p. 10.
[18] Ibid, p. 13.

Skills inventory and training program records
Insurance claims
Security records
Performance evaluations
Promotion tables

Management decisions based on employment records, such as the set outlined here, can therefore be classed as follows:

Selection and placement decisions
Developmental decisions (transfer, promotion, demotion, and training)
Discipline
Administration of employee benefits
Separation

Management use of personnel information

In analyzing employee records, the Privacy Protection Study Commission recognized a strong trend away from formal, rule-bound procedures for personnel decisionmaking. It also noted the absence of a general framework of rights and obligations that should ordinarily accompany a sophisticated computer-based personnel system, such as the systems maintained by many large organizations.

The commission therefore developed two general recommendations:

Absence of adequate procedures

Recommendation (1):

That an employer periodically and systematically examine its employment and personnel record-keeping practices, including a review of:

(a) the number and types of records it maintains on individual employees, former employees, and applicants;
(b) the items of information contained in each type of employment record it maintains;
(c) the uses made of the items of information in each type of record;
(d) the uses made of such records within the employing organization;
(e) the disclosures made of such records to parties outside the employing organization; and
(f) the extent to which individual employees, former employees, and applicants are both aware and systematically in-

Recommendations concerning a framework of rights and obligations

formed of the uses and disclosures that are made of information in the records kept about them.[19]

Recommendation (2):

That an employer articulate, communicate, and implement fair
information practice policies for employment records which
should include:

(a) limiting the collection of information on individual employees, former employees, and applicants to that which is
relevant to specific decisions;
(b) informing employees, applicants, and former employees
who maintain a continuing relationship with the employer
of the uses to be made of such information;
(c) informing employees as to the types of records that are being maintained on them;
(d) adopting reasonable procedures to assure the accuracy,
timeliness, and completeness of information collected,
maintained, used, or disclosed about individual employees,
former employees, and applicants;
(e) permitting individual employees, former employees, and
applicants to see, copy, correct, or amend the records maintained about them;
(f) limiting the internal use of records maintained on individual
employees, former employees, and applicants;
(g) limiting external disclosures of information in records kept
on individual employees, former employees, and applicants,
including disclosures made without the employee's authorization in response to specific inquiries or requests to verify
information about him; and
(h) providing for regular review of compliance with articulated
fair information practice policies.[20]

**Considerations apply
to large organizations**

Of course, the analysis of employment records relates
primarily to large organizations, since recordkeeping is more
important when management can only deal with a small
number of individuals on a personal basis. Almost all large
organizations use computer-based personnel systems. The
total amount of information about individual employees that
is stored in such a system does not seem to have been increased relative to a manual personnel system. Nevertheless,
the easy accessibility of information through data base and

**"Need-to-know"
policy needed**

[19] Ibid, p. 36.
[20] Ibid, pp. 42–43.

communications systems suggests that a "need-to-know" policy is necessary in order to control the disclosure of personnel records.

SUMMARY

Data protection in computer-based information systems is a complex topic, involving legal and moral issues that reach beyond the scope of traditional recordkeeping systems. Data protection and data regulation are related to the notion of privacy. Privacy has been defined by Westin as *the claim of individuals, groups, or institutions to determine for themselves when, how, and to what extent information about them is communicated to others.* The normal functions served by privacy should be an integral part of an effective data protection program. However, it is impossible to control the behavior of individuals—regardless of the level of security provided by modern computer systems. A worthwhile objective of an effective data protection plan would be the establishment of legal sanctions that would guarantee autonomy of choice in certain private areas so that persons would have less to fear even if information about them were more widely accessible.

Privacy safeguards are a defense against the gradual trend toward ignoring the individual's need for privacy. A person can lose control of information about himself or herself in three ways:

1. Information is obtained against a subject's wishes.
2. Information is obtained from an agency against the wishes of the agency and the subject.
3. Information is willingly disclosed by the beneficial user or agency but against the subject's wishes.

Some of the most obvious considerations in providing privacy safeguards are:

1. Information that is not collected does not have to be protected.
2. Unneeded information should be destroyed.
3. Inaccurate information should be corrected or destroyed.
4. The level of danger of disclosure of information is re-

lated to the amount of private information that persons supply to recordkeepers.

5. Some restrictions should exist on the kinds of information that certain organizations should possess.

Recordkeeping, which is an important function of society, normally includes three types of records about people: administrative, intelligence, and statistical. In most modern computer-based information systems, recordkeeping activities cannot be neatly placed in any one of these categories, and some overlap exists.

Certain traditions exist relative to government records about people; these traditions are reflected as a set of five principles concerning safeguards for automated personal-data systems. Appendixes A and B give sets of safeguard requirements for administrative personal-data systems and statistical reporting and research systems, respectively.

One of the most ambitious and far-reaching approaches to the protection of personal data is the Privacy Act of 1974. The act includes a variety of procedural requirements for federal agencies ranging from annual reporting in the *Federal Register* to the administration of the provisions of the act. The substance of the Privacy Act is summarized in eight basic principles:

- Openness
- Individual Access
- Individual Participation
- Collection Limitation
- Use Limitation
- Disclosure Limitation
- Information Management
- Accountability

The protection of personal-data systems has turned out to be more complex than anticipated, and the act does not satisfactorily resolve all policy issues. The real danger, as stated in the report of the Privacy Protection Study Commission, lies in the interconnection of small, separate recordkeeping systems.

Two important classes of recordkeeping activities that affect the day-to-day life of most individuals are tax and employment records. These records normally contain a substantial amount of personal information that an individual would probably not otherwise disclose.

IMPORTANT TERMS AND CONCEPTS

The reader should be familiar with the following terms and concepts:

Accountability principle
Administrative records
Collection Limitation Principle
Compelled self-disclosure
Consent to giving information
Disclosure as a condition
Disclosure Limitation Principle
Electronic surveillance
Freedom of Information Act
Individual Access Principle
Individual Participation Principle
Information Management Principle
Informers and secret agents
Intelligence records
Observation and permanent recording
Openness Principle
Participant monitoring
Privacy
Privacy Act of 1974
Searches and seizure
Statistical records
Use Limitation Principle

READINGS AND REFERENCES

Greenawalt, K. *Legal Protections of Privacy*. Final Report to the Office of Telecommunications Policy, Executive Office of the President. Washington, D.C.: U.S. Government Printing Office, Stock No. 041-001-00105-1, 1975.

Katzan, H., Jr. *Computer Data Security*. New York: Van Nostrand Reinhold Company, 1973.

Larsen, K. S., ed. *Privacy, A Public Concern*. Proceedings of a Seminar on Privacy, sponsored by The Domestic Council Committee on the Right of Privacy and The Council of State Governments. Washington, D.C.: U.S. Government Printing Office, 1975.

Miller, A. R. *The Assault on Privacy: Computers, Data Banks, and Dossiers*. Ann Arbor, Michigan: The University of Michigan Press, 1971.

National Information Policy. Report to the President of the United States submitted by the Staff of the Domestic Council Committee on the Right of Privacy. Washington, D.C.: U.S. Government Printing Office, Stock No. 052–003–00296–5, 1976.

Records, Computers, and the Rights of Citizens, Report of the Secretary's Advisory Committee on Automated Personal Data Systems, U.S. Department of Health, Education, and Welfare. Cambridge, Massachusetts: M.I.T. Press, 1973.

The Report of the Privacy Protection Study Commission, July 1977. Available from the Superintendent of Documents, U.S. Government Printing Office, Washington, D.C. 20402.

- *Personal Privacy in an Information Society,* Stock No. 052–003–00395–6.
- Appendix 1, *Privacy Law in the States,* Stock No. 052–003–00395–6.
- Appendix 2, *The Citizen as Taxpayer,* Stock No. 052–003–00422–4.
- Appendix 3, *Employment Records,* Stock No. 052–003–00423–2.
- Appendix 4, *The Privacy Act of 1974: An Assessment,* Stock No. 052–003–00424–1.
- Appendix 5, *Technology and Privacy,* Stock No. 052–003–00425–9.

Rosenberg, J. M. *The Death of Privacy.* New York: Random House, 1969.

Turn, R. Classification of personal information for privacy protection purposes. *Proceedings of the 1976 National Computer Conference* (1976), AFIPS Vol. 45, pp. 301–307.

Ware, W. H. Handling personal data, *Datamation* (October 1977), pp. 83–87.

Westin, A. E. *Computers, Health Records, and Citizen's Rights.* Princeton, New Jersey: PBI—Petrocelli Books, 1977.

5

APPROACHES AND ACTIVITIES IN DATA REGULATION AND TRANSBORDER DATA FLOW

For this is a matter of cold, hard, inescapable fact: telecommunications is the inevitable result of all man's history, all his efforts to deal with and to improve his environment and his life in his environment—all tools, all learning, every technique man ever devised to learn, to retain, to pass on his knowledge—his lifelong, billion-year-old struggle to gather, store, analyze and transmit data have led us to this most efficient means of all—telecommunications.

JOHN M. EGER

The present concern over data regulation and transborder data flow is partially due to the rapid changes in computer and communications technology. Advances have occurred so rapidly that existing domestic and international institutions are unable to cope with them. The new technology has created a need for a global information policy since the level of international interdependence has increased substantially. Clearly, this is not solely a technical or even a legal issue. All issues merge into one when the concern is over information policy. Interrelated issues that have been identified thus far include economic capability, privacy, information isolation, human rights, and national sovereignty.

Global information policy

Several organizations, such as the Organization for Eco-

Table 5-1.   Status of National Privacy/Data Protection Legislation as of January 1979.

Legislation Enacted

Austria (1978)	Germany (1977)
Canada (1978)	Norway (1978)
Denmark (1978)	Sweden (1973)
France (1978)	United States (1974)

Legislation before Parliament

Belgium	Netherlands
Luxembourg	Spain

Government Report Awaiting Implementation

United Kingdom

Government Reports in Preparation

Australia	Japan
Finland	New Zealand
Iceland	Switzerland
Italy	

Source: Pipe, G. R. Status of national privacy/data protection legislation as of January 1979. *Computerworld* (February 12, 1979). Copyright 1979 by CW Communications/Inc. Newton, Mass. 02160—Reprinted from COMPUTERWORLD.

Several international organizations and various countries are concerned with data regulation

nomic Cooperation and Development (OECD) and the Council of Europe, are concerned with data regulation and transborder data flow. Also, several countries, such as Austria, Sweden, and the United States have enacted national privacy or data protection legislation. Table 5-1 gives the status of such legislation as of January 1979.

OVERVIEW OF INTERNATIONAL ACTIVITY

Laws have been enacted that could affect multinational computer systems

Objectives are personal privacy and economic and political issues

Several international legislatures have enacted privacy and/or data protection laws governing personal data, which could affect the design and operation of multinational computer systems. The laws effectively encompass transborder data flow and may be extended in the future to include legal persons, such as corporations. On the surface, the objective of such laws is to protect personal privacy through systems of licensing and registration; the underlying objectives are sometimes economic and political.

Herbert E. Marks of the law firm of Wilkinson, Cragun

and Barker has summarized the issues well in a recent article.[1] Some of the factors contributing to data regulation legislation are:

1. Information is becoming more important to technically advanced societies.
2. Internation communications are becoming easier.
3. More attention is being given to privacy and human rights.
4. Computer systems facilitate the collection, storage, processing, and retrieval of information.
5. The advantages of computer facilities are enhanced through remote-access capability.

Factors contributing to data regulation legislation

Legislative trends for various countries are covered in more detail later in this chapter. Following is a summary of features present in current European legislation, resulting from an effort to resolve the preceding factors:[2]

1. There is an emphasis on regulation of the private sector.
2. Legislation normally applies to collected data that are name-linked.
3. Legislation frequently applies only to data that are stored, processed, and retrieved through the use of an electronic computer.
4. Legislation applies to collected personal data in general and not to a specific class of data.
5. Licensing or registration is the usual method of enforcement.
6. Governmental organizations are established to provide enforcement.
7. The data processing ''agency'' that supplies a service function is frequently regulated as well as the ''beneficial user.''
8. Legislation normally contains provisions governing data that are processed outside of the host country, as well as internally to the host country.

Features present in current European legislation

[1] Marks, H. E. Crossborder data nets become targets of European lawmakers. *Data Communications* (September 1978), pp. 67–68. Reprinted from *Data Communications*. Copyright 1978. McGraw-Hill Inc. All rights reserved.
[2] *Ibid,* p. 68.

9. Legislation effectively provides the host government, through the licensing or registration provisions of the law, with a master list of all data collected and of data files that contain personal data.

Unilateral efforts may not be the answer to the total problem

Looking at the total data regulation picture, it is doubtful that the development of legislation on a unilateral basis will derive the desired results—or any useful result at all. In fact, it may be difficult to delineate the expected or desired results because of diverse legislative processes. The situation was summarized well by John M. Eger, former head of the White House Office of Telecommunications Policy, in an address before the Conference on Transnational Data Regulation:

Picket-fence legislation

We may thus be faced with incompatible regulation—a set of restrictions which, taken together, will resemble a picket fence or information curtain; the laws of one country standing rigidly with those of all the others to effectively inhibit if not bar the transnational flow of information.[3]

More specifically, the possible effects of this patchwork of laws, as identified by Herbert Marks, are:

Effects of a patchwork of laws

- Use of EDP will become more expensive because it may be necessary for users to make longer, more costly communications line detours around certain countries to avoid restrictions. Also, where an operation may be located in a restrictive nation and have to be cut out of a network, communications volume will decline—resulting in higher costs per call for the remaining users.
- Penalties for innocent violations of complex regulations will discourage use of EDP.
- Multinational data processing companies will be facing compliance with disparate regulatory patterns, and higher costs of doing business because of limited data flow from some countries.
- Countries that unduly regulate data processing may be left with limited access to international networks—in both the services they offer and the information databases they contain.
- All countries will suffer if the development of transnational data processing networks, offering computer services and

[3] Eger, J. M. The Brussels Mandate: An Alliance for the Future of World Communications and Information Policy, p. 7. Address before the Conference on Transnational Data Regulation, Brussels, Belgium, February 9, 1978. Courtesy of The Brussels Mandate, Washington, D.C.

databases to virtually any location at the lowest possible cost, are inhibited.

- Cost to any nation of impeding the free flow of information will be reflected in the cost of available goods and services, because computer services are not end products.

Negative aspects of data regulation

- Individuals will suffer if the use of personal data is curtailed so as to limit employment, travel opportunities, and other legitimate use of such data.

- The economic viability of public packet-switched data networks, planned for various countries, will be affected. Network vitality will depend in part on the ease with which data flows back and forth across national borders.[4]

The negative aspects of data regulation are clearly evident.

Although the current interest in data regulation may seem to be of recent origin, the concern of Europeans over human rights and privacy is long-established. It is inherent in the activities of such organizations as UNESCO, the OECD, and the Council of Europe, to cite only a few. UNESCO has several projects in the area of data regulation; Appendix D contains two resolutions on the subject adopted by the Twentieth General Conference of UNESCO. The OECD has been involved in a variety of data regulation projects. Appendix E contains proposed guidelines to the OECD submitted by the United States and an apparent response to that submission by the OECD Secretariat. Similarly, the Council of Europe has been heavily engaged in data protection and the broader issue of human rights. Appendix F contains the Council's preliminary draft of an International Convention on the Protection of Individuals Vis-à-Vis Automated Records. Appendix G presents the Council's document, "The European Convention on Human Rights."

Concern over human rights is not of recent origin

UNESCO, OECD, and the Council of Europe are all active

OECD ACTIVITY

The OECD is concerned with advances in information technology and associated international policy implications. Recognizing that the combination of computer and communications technology is a valuable national resource, the OECD has been investigating six avenues:

OECD recognizes that information technology is a valuable national resource

1. Legal implications of transnational data flow
2. Characterization of problems as national or international in dimension

[4] Marks, H. E., op. cit., pp. 68–69.

Six areas being investigated by the OECD

3. Methods of international cooperation—bilateral or multilateral
4. Economics of transnational data flow and the pricing of communications
5. The growth of data services
6. Implications for national sovereignty

Clearly, the OECD's emphasis is on the vulnerability of society as it is related to national economies and the interdependence of nations.

One of the major achievements of the OECD in the area of transnational data flow was the establishment in January 1977 of the Working Party on Information, Computer and Communications Policy. This group enabled the OECD to adopt a broader perspective on transnational data flow and was the force behind the Vienna Symposium on Transborder Data Flows and the Protection of Privacy in September 1977. The overall conclusions that were drawn from the symposium were:

OECD policy group

(i) national and international issues arising from the rapid extension of data networks are closely related, and must in future be considered in the same overall framework;

(ii) their legal aspects, concerned with the protection of personal privacy, cannot be divorced from the economic and political aspects relating to the free flow of information, and they must be considered internationally;

Conclusions of the Vienna symposium

(iii) the rapid development of information and communication technologies, and the decrease in their cost, are accelerating the creation and use of data networks to such an extent that the existing organisational and legal framework will have to be overhauled;

(iv) if obstacles to the international flow of essential, largely non-personal data, are to be avoided, national legislation concerning the privacy of personal data demand international co-ordination and harmonisation, based on commonly accepted guiding principles;

(v) in view of the economic nature of the work of OECD, and its membership, OECD has an important role to play in helping Member countries to deal with these issues.[5]

One result of the symposium was the establishment of a

[5] Gassman, H. P. The activities of OECD in the field of transnational data regulation. In *Data Regulation: European and Third World Realities,* Proceedings of the Online Conference, p. 181. New York, November 1978.

High-level Expert Group on Transborder Data Barriers. The aim of the group was to develop guidelines for bridging the privacy-protection legislation now developing in many European countries and similar legislation being developed in non-European OECD member countries.

High-level expert group

COUNCIL OF EUROPE

The Council of Europe's mandate in data protection was given by its Consultative Assembly as follows:

> In its Recommendation 509 (1968) it asked for a study into the question whether the right to privacy, as protected in national law and under Article 8 of the European Human Rights Convention, was likely to suffer interferences as a result of the development of modern technology. In response to this recommendation, the Council of Europe's intergovernmental branch, the Committee of Ministers, set up a Committee of experts which reported in 1971. The Committee found that the use of modern record-keeping techniques and especially computers raised problems which were not satisfactorily answered by the Human Rights Convention or by domestic legislation. With regard to the Convention it pointed out that this instrument was concerned only with the relationship between the State and the individual and afforded no protection to individuals with regard to record keeping in the private sector. Moreover, further guidelines were needed in view of the provisions of Article 10 of the same Convention, guaranteeing freedom of information. A balance should be struck between the conflicting claims of an individual, the community, and other individuals with regard to the gathering, processing and use of personal information.[6]

Council of Europe's mandate in data protection

In response, the Council developed a set of resolutions that would apply to governments. These resolutions are concerned with the following safeguards concerning recordkeeping:

- Accuracy
- Physical data security
- Fair collection of information
- Rights of the data subject
- Control of the use of information
- Integrity of computer personnel

Resolutions applying to governments on the subject of data regulation

[6] Hondius, F. W. "The Council of Europe's data protection principles," p. 49. Extract from the proceedings of an Online Conferences Ltd. conference and the subsequently published *Transnational Data Regulation: The Realities* (1979).

Real costs of data regulation

Recognizing the "omnibus" nature of European laws, Dr. Frits W. Hondius, head of the Division of Public Law of the Council of Europe, assesses that the real cost of these safeguards to commercial organizations arises from the obligation (1) to file statements, applications, and reports with supervisory bodies, and (2) to respond to interventions by data subjects, and (3) to meet costs of administration and civil litigation. Furthermore, the costs may be offset by indirect benefits, such as discovering flaws in an agency's system. Finally, Hondius believes that the increased transparency of recordkeeping in the commercial sector may result in the loss of business opportunity.[7]

Indirect benefits

VIEWPOINT FROM AUSTRIA

A view of international regulation on data flow and privacy protection from Austria is presented in international conferences by Dr. Gerhard Stadler, head of department a.i. in the Austrian prime minister's office. Dr. Stadler, an international authority on data regulation, is responsible for the preparation of the Austrian Privacy Act. He was a member of the Working Groups of the Council of Europe on the subject of information in law and was appointed to the Chair of the OECD Data Bank Panel.

Protection against the negative consequences of modern information technology

The underlying objective of Austrian data regulation is to protect against the negative consequences of modern information technologies. The law protects the exchange of information by electronic methods and is not intended to apply to manual information systems although manual recordkeeping may be affected.

The Austrian data protection law is based on three common principles:

Common principles of data protection

- a relation between the collection of data and their use should be obligatory
- the person concerned must basically be offered the possibility to have access to his or her data and to correct them in case they are wrong or to erase obsolete information or information obtained in an unlawful way
- a supervisory authority is planned which may either intervene directly in data processing (Sweden: systems of permissions)

[7] Ibid., p. 54.

or at least observe the development and point out misuses (FRA, USA) to give advice for further political actions.[8]

The goals of the law is threefold: to prevent the evasion of national data provisions by the export of data abroad, to protect citizens by the national legislation when data are used abroad, and to prevent the existence of "pirate data band" in countries without sufficient data protection.[9]

International activity

The essence of the Austrian data protection law is summarized by Dr. Stadler as follows:

> The *Austrian* bill of 1975 only allows data processing for Austrian companies in foreign countries, if the principles of Austrian law are kept safe. The amendment of this bill, which is now discussed by a Committee of the Parliament in the meantime, intends furthermore to make data processing for Austrian companies abroad subject to the consent of the Data Protection Commission. This authority should give the permission for transfrontier data traffic when it is foreseen in an international agreement or in the importing state [that] data protection regulations similar to the Austrian's are in force.[10]

Overview of the Austrian law

The Austrian law is summarized by G. Russell Pipe, an international data regulation consultant, as follows:

- Applies to public and private sectors.
- Applies to DP and some manual files.
- Creates a regulatory agency.
- Establishes a registry of personal files.
- Requires personal data to be collected by lawful and fair means and to be kept accurate.
- Requires that personal data be kept confidential, that their secondary use be controlled, that external transfers be logged, and that security measures be adopted.
- Sets penalties for violations.
- Conditions transborder data flows.

Summary of the Austrian law

---

[8] Stadler, G. To international regulations on data flows and privacy protection p. 98. Extract from the proceedings of an Online Conferences Ltd. conference and the subsequently published *Transnational Data Regulation: The Realities* (1979).
[9] Ibid., p. 100.
[10] Ibid., p. 99.

- Gives data subjects the right to be informed or otherwise notified of personal data stored, to have access to their files, and to get erroneous information corrected or deleted.[11]

VIEWPOINT FROM SWEDEN

Swedish Data Act complements a freedom of the press act

In 1973, Sweden became the first nation to enact nationwide personal privacy legislation. The Swedish Data Act was designed to complement a comprehensive Freedom of the Press Act, which guarantees public access to all public documents—including information that is entered on a computer input medium.

Data Inspection Board

An integral part of the Swedish Data Act is the Data Inspection Board, which is empowered to grant licenses to perform recordkeeping of personal-data files and to monitor compliance with the act. Permission of the board must be obtained by anyone wishing to set up a data file containing personal data about data subjects. In granting a license, the board reviews the kind and quantity of personal data to be

Licensing

stored in addition to other social factors. The decision to grant a license is based on whether there is reason to assume that undue infringement of the registered person's privacy will arise. Moreover, personal files that apply to a substanial part of the total population or region are permitted only if

Relationship with the beneficial agency

the subjects (1) have an accepted relationship to the beneficial agency, such as employee or customer, (2) if the subjects provide consent, or (3) if special circumstances are present. Special considerations also apply to files containing medical, religious, or political data and to the handling of incorrect data.

Provisions of the Swedish Data Act

The Swedish Data Act provides for notification of the data subjects and the specification of the conditions under which personal data may be released to external data processing agencies for processing abroad. The act also covers installation management principles and compliance monitoring. In the latter category, the Data Inspection Board is entitled to inspect computer installations and to made arrangements for special computer runs to insure that personal privacy is not infringed upon.

Punitive provisions

The Swedish Data Act contains punitive provisions that in-

---

[11] Pipe, G. R. Three nations to pass privacy laws in '79, more may follow suit. *Computerworld* (February 12, 1979), p. 20.

clude fines, imprisonment, and compensatory measures for subjects suffering a loss through privacy violations.

VIEWPOINT FROM GERMANY

A viewpoint on data protection from the Federal Republic of Germany is represented by Dr. R. Schomerus, a member of the staff of the Office of the Federal Data Protection Commissioner. The Federal Data Protection Act of the Federal Republic of Germany, which became effective on January 1, 1978, applies to personal data stored in electronic data banks, as well as to manual data banks. However, manually stored data that are *not* transmitted to third parties are exempted from the law. Legal persons are not protected by the German law.

German law applies to electronic and manual data banks

The objective of the Federal Data Protection Act is to protect the citizen and not specifically to protect the actual data. However, the practicalities of individual protection have dictated that the method of implementation be a data protection law concerned with the rights of privacy inherent in the storage of and access to personal data. The German law has a broad scope and applies to both the federal administration and private business. Excluding federal states, which are expected to implement their own data protection laws, the law applies to all organizations that process personal data, such as banks, insurance companies, manufacturing organizations, and sociopolitical groups. Of interest here is that the law

Objective: protect the citizen

German law applies to all organizations that process personal data—federal and private

. . . applies to physical and legal persons and other private law associations

- which store and process personal data for the purposes of communication to third parties, i.e., credit reporting agencies, direct-mailing-firms,
- further to enterprises which collect data, anonymise them and communicate the results to third parties, e.g. market research and opinion poll institutes,
- and thirdly to enterprises, which process data in the normal course of business as service on behalf of third parties."[12]

Organizations affected

The basis of the Federal Data Protection Act is the ex-

[12] Schomerus, R. The German Federal Data Protection Act. In *Data Regulation: European and Third World Realities,* Proceedings of the Online Conference. p. 87. New York, November 1978.

Contractual relationship between parties

istence of a contractual relationship between the data subject and the beneficial user. When an explicit or an implicit contract exists between the parties, as in the case of an employer-employee relationship, personal data may be stored if there is no reason to suppose that the interests of the data subject will be harmed. Certain specific personal data, such as name, address, date of birth, occupation, and telephone number, may be communicated freely provided that no harm will ensue to the data subject.

Interests of the data subject

Blocked data, verification, and erasure

Personal data that are proved to be incorrect, or that cannot be verified as being correct when contested by the data subject, are "blocked," which means that they cannot be further used or transmitted. Moreover, when the lawful need for maintaining personal data ceases to exist, the data are blocked, and erasure can be requested by the data subject. Data dealing with sensitive issues such as health, criminal offenses, and religious and political information must be erased if it cannot be verified.

One level of protection is inherent in the subject—the right of access

The philosophical basis for the German law lies in the contention that the first level of data protection is inherent in the actions of the data subject. Therefore, through the "right of access," a data subject has the right to know what data about him or her are stored, and where. The data subject is informed of the storage of relevant data in one of several ways. First, federal agencies must publish the following information in the official gazette:

- Type of data stored
- Tasks for which the stored data are needed
- Group of persons affected
- Agencies to which the data will be transmitted on a regular basis
- Type of data transmitted

Official notification

In addition, private organizations that store and process personal data for their own internal use must insure that the data subject is cognizant of the storage. These provisions also apply to organizations that process data on behalf of others,* such as service bureaus and credit-reporting bureaus. In the latter case, the data subject can request the erasure of data up to five years after storage.

---

* Referred to earlier as the "agency."

Enforcement is achieved through a system of representatives, empowered to control, monitor, and inspect data banks containing personal data. At the federal level, a *federal commissioner* is appointed to insure compliance; at the state level, supervisory boards are designated for the same purpose. In the private sector, data protection representatives are required for organizations that exceed a minimal level and store personal data. Penalties for unauthorized communication of or modification to personal data include fines and imprisonment.

Enforcement and monitoring

The Federal Data Protection Act does not specifically cover transborder flows; however, it is generally regarded that international data transfer is effectively covered under the act. In cases wherein international laws and agreements do not apply, the following prerequisites of permissibility, included in the federal law, are commonly considered:

Extension of the federal data protection law to transborder data flow

According to the first alternative, personal data may be communicated by federal authorities if it is necessary for the legitimate accomplishment of the tasks incumbent upon the communicating unit. This will hardly ever be the case without a special legal basis.

Permissibility of transborder data flow

According to the second alternative, such data may be communicated, "where the recipient can demonstrate convincingly that his interest in the data to be communicated is justified and that the communication of the data does not harm any interests of the person concerned that warrant protection." It will be relatively easy for a potential recipient to demonstrate convincingly that a justified interest exists on his part; nevertheless it will have to be assumed that, in all cases where no data protection legislation exists in the recipient country, there is reason to suppose that interests of the person concerned warranting protection will be harmed. In such cases the data can only be communicated under aggravated conditions and, in the final analysis, only with the consent of the person concerned.[13]

The German law clearly recognizes that a considerable amount of the international transfer of personal data involves information on employees of multinational organizations—a case clearly covered by the inherent contractual or quasi-contractual relationship.

International data transfer

[13] Ibid., p. 222. Extract from the proceedings of an Online Conferences Ltd. conference and the subsequently published *Transnational Data Regulation: The Realities* (1979).

VIEWPOINT FROM FRANCE

French law is multidimensional and applies to natural persons

The French privacy and data protection law, which covers only natural persons, was made a public law on January 6, 1978. It took partial effect on January 1, 1979, and was totally in force as of January 1, 1980. The law is multidimensional in the sense that it applies to all data base categories. The establishing of public data bases requires prior authorization, whereas the creation of a data base in the private sector requires only prior declaration.

The French law is similar to that of other European jurisdictions. It guarantees minimum protection through the following general provisions:

Provisions of the French law

1. Establishment of a control body
2. Widespread publicity of data bases
3. Appropriate regulations concerning the gathering of data

In addition, the French law covers safety measures for data protection, the regulation of international data flow, and the right of access and rectification.

Enforcement

Enforcement is achieved through the National Commission for Data Processing and Freedoms, which advises the data processing industry on all aspects of data processing and individual freedom and insures the effective supervision of both public and private data files.

Control of data use is achieved in the following manner:

There is one interesting new element intended to draw the attention of individual citizens to the phenomena of data processing. It is intended to encourage everyone who receives a questionnaire to think before he answers it. It will, therefore, be obligatory when personal data is being collected to inform the data subject:

Control of data

i)   If his reply is optional or compulsory
ii) Where it is compulsory, what are the consequences of a refusal to reply
iii) What is the specific destination of the information collected
iv) To advise of the existence of a right of access

The second characteristic is that there are measures which prohibit the registration of certain specific data. The two most important categories are what might be called sensitive personal data such as those relating to our religious, political or trade union affiliations.[14]

The extension of the French law to manual data bases is unique. It is summarized in the following list:

1. The rules (prior authorisation or declaration) applying automatic data bases should not apply to manual data bases

2. the basic rules (prohibition from recording discriminatory information—individual right of access, etc.) should apply in return to manual data bases

    Manual data bases

3. multicopying data bases should be put on the same footing as manual data bases

4. decrees could, in the light of experience, decide that the rules of form will apply to certain particularly sensitive manual data bases[15]

Clearly, the provisions concerning manual data bases were formulated in light of the large number of manual data bases and the exercise of individual liberty.

VIEWPOINT FROM CANADA

While personal privacy and human rights are important issues in Canada, the major issue is economic. This opinion was voiced by Dr. Peter Robinson of the Department of Communications, when he stated that

    Major issue is economic

the principal problem is not one of the privacy of Canadian data subjects being invaded by data about them being stored in the United States, but rather that data processing and communications business may be lost to Canadians as a result of this foreign flow.[16]

    Business loss to Canada

This is not a clear-cut issue in Canada since certain "economies of scale" are inherent in centralized computing, and the high cost of data processing in Canada would encourage centralized computing in the United States. For

[14] Joinet, L. Transcript of ad hoc presentation. In *Transnational Data Regulation,* Proceedings of the Online Conference, p. 279. Brussels, February 1978.
[15] Joinet, L. French law in relation to information privacy. In *Data Regulation: European and Third World Realities,* Proceedings of the Online Conference, p. 219. New York, November 1978.
[16] Economic and dependency issues overshadow privacy in Canadian/U.S. data flow talks. *Transnational Data Report* (November 1978), Vol. 1, No. 5, p. 2.

Centralization and economy of scale

United States–based organizations, there is also a tendency to centralize in the parent company, especially when costs are lower. Nevertheless, national boundaries do exist, and a comprehensive study of the long-term effects of data regulation among technologically advanced nations is badly needed.

Human Rights Act

Privacy legislation in Canada is inherent in the Human Rights Act, which was passed in July 1977. One part of the law specifically deals with personal information stored by noncommercial federal government departments and institutions. The law is based on the following basic rights:

The right *to know* what records that are used for administrative purposes, are held by a federal department or institution concerning an individual.

Basic rights

The right *to know the uses* to which such information has been put since 1 March 1978.

The right *to examine* such personal information as well as the right *to challenge* the correctness, completeness, relevancy and currency of that information and to require a notation on a file when a correction is not accepted.

The right to be consulted in respect of proposed *non-derivative uses* for administrative purposes, of information provided to the federal government by an individual.[17]

The Canadian Human Rights Act gives the individual the following rights regarding personal data:

(a) to ascertain what records concerning the individual inquiring are used for administrative purposes and are contained in banks listed in an index published by the federal government;

(b) to ascertain the uses to which such information has been put *since* the proclamation of Part IV which took place on the 1st of March 1978;

Rights regarding personal data

(c) to examine such records or copies thereof, regardless of who provided the information; and

(d) to request correction of the personal information; or

(e) to require a notation on the record if the correction is not accepted.[18]

[17] Hansen, I. National Privacy Concerns and Action—Canada at the Federal level. Unpublished presentation, p. 1 (November 1978).
[18] Ibid., p. 2.

An important definition is that of the *individual,* which is defined as "a Canadian" or "a person lawfully admitted to Canada for permanent residence." **Individual**

Certain exemptions to "access and correction" rights exist, which involve federal-provincial agreements of confidentiality, international relations, national security, and criminal affairs. In general, exemptions to the right of access and correction are permitted if, in the opinion of the minister of justice, the disclosure:

(a) might be injurious to international relations, national defence, national security, or federal-provincial relations

(b) would disclose a confidence of the Queen's Privy Council (Cabinet secret)

(c) would be likely to disclose information obtained by a federal investigatory body in relation to national security, during investigations pertaining to (i) detection or suppression of crime or (ii) the administration and enforcement of any **Exemptions to** federal statute **access and**

(d) in respect of a person under sentence, if disclosure might **correction rights** lead to a serious disruption of that individual's institutional parole, or mandatory supervision program, reveal information that was originally obtained on an implied or express promise of confidentiality, or result in physical or other harm to the person under sentence or to any other person,

or if disclosure

(e) might reveal personal information concerning another individual

(f) might impede the functioning of a court of law, a quasi- **Result of disclosure** judicial board, commission or other tribunal under the Inquiries Act

(g) might disclose legal opinion or advice to a government institution, or privileged communications between lawyer and client in a matter of government business.[19]

To insure that there are no secret personal information banks, all federal departments and institutions must list all personal information banks, excluding the exemptions just presented. The provisions of the law are administered by a privacy commissioner, who is empowered to investigate all complaints from individuals who claim that their privacy rights have been violated.

[19] Ibid., p. 3.

With regard to national sovereignty and the national economy, Dr. Robinson analyzed the flow of data across national boundaries and established four general categories of data:

Categories of data

1. Business transaction
2. Public
3. Personal
4. Corporate

Dr. Robinson concluded that regulation of data in the first and second categories would be unlikely to benefit the host nation for obvious reasons related to international trade. However, the third and fourth categories

present some worrisome aspects, and may require some type of controls of reciprocal arrangements. I believe that the actual transfer *per se* is not the major problem: it is what is done with the data *after* transfer that may give rise to a number of problems.

Result of disclosure of personal or corporate data

In the case of personal data, its unauthorized disclosure could lead to embarrassment, or in some cases perhaps to loss of job; or sale of mailing lists could lead to an increase in junk mail to particular individuals; or some use other than that for which it was originally collected may cause other problems. In the case of corporate data, the wholesale export of detailed data on the day-to-day operations of a company for processing and storage abroad could have significant impacts on employment and on balance of payments. In addition, the concomitant transfer of management and control functions, made possible by the technological developments, reduces further the ability of Canadians to control significant developments in Canada. The transfer of corporate data could further jeopardize Canadian jurisdiction over companies operating within Canada.[20]

Even though there are two sides to every coin, it is evident that the issues are complex and the long-term implications of data regulation are substantial.

[20] Robinson, P. Strategic Issues Related to Transborder Data Flow. Notes for a presentation to the Online International Conference on Data Regulation, p. 3. New York, November 1978. Extract from the proceedings of an Online Conferences Ltd. conference and the subsequently published *Transnational Data Regulation: The Realities* (1979).

CONSIDERATIONS IN DEVELOPING COUNTRIES

To some developing countries, *informatics,* the systematic planning and utilization of data processing facilities, is a tool of nationalism, as it can be employed to reduce dependency on the services of other nations. Because of the lead time necessary to develop an effective data processing capability, many developing countries are deficient with regard to:

Informatics is a tool of nationalism

1. Availability of qualified personnel
2. Existence of planning on overall economic development
3. A development plan for a national computer policy
4. Training and experience in computers and in data processing

Deficiencies in developing countries

One method of solving the problem in a developing nation is to create a central organization responsible for establishing a set of national data processing objectives and associated plans and policies. After the plan was implemented, the same organization would be responsible for monitoring and controlling it.

Central organization for planning

One method of achieving data processing independence is to control transborder data flow that offers computing and information services. This opinion is summarized by Ricardo A. C. Saur, executive secretary of CAPRE, Brazil's Coordinating Committee for EDP Activities:

Data processing independence

> We believe, therefore, that there exists a need for protection of local development efforts, since "competition" is not going to be achieved because of (a) disparities in the development stage not related to the technology in question (b) indirect or even direct "dumping" practices derived from already paid development costs, more often than not having been originally projects funded by defense contracts or government-sponsored research (c) greater financial help from international banks or local interdependent banks that offer special conditions (d) smaller sales volumes because the international market on high-technology products is closed to non-members of the interdependent's group.[21]

Need for protection

[21] Saur, R. A. C. Informatics, new technologies and data regulation: a view from the Third World. In *Data Regulation: European and Third World Realities,* Proceedings of the Online Conference, p. 224. New York, November 1978. Extract from the proceedings of an Online Conferences Ltd. conference and the subsequently published *Transnational Data Regulation: The Realities* (1979).

Thus, in Saur's opinion, protection is needed to bridge the dependence gap. Others believe that protection can partially answer questions regarding transnational data flow, such as:

Protection can eliminate serious problems

1. How should problems resulting from the interruption of telecommunications links be alleviated?
2. How can the "leakage" of information be avoided?

Clearly, the need for protection is a blend of economic and political issues. Indeed, in a developing country, the eventual solution of the protection situation relates to whether that nation can afford the resources necessary to develop a national computer and data processing capability in light of other pressing problems.

Protection is a blend of economic and political issues

RECENT UNITED STATES ACTIVITY

Recent activity to protect the privacy of individuals in the United States is summarized in a message to the Congress delivered in April 1979 by President Carter.[22]

I am announcing today sweeping proposals to protect the privacy of individuals.

"The right to be let alone," Justice Brandeis wrote 60 years ago, "is the right most valued by civilized men." That right is built into our Constitution, which forbids unwarranted searches of citizens and their homes. At the time the Constitution was written—a time when private conversations were conducted face-to-face or through the mail and most private records were kept at home—those protections seemed adequate.

Justice Brandeis

The growth of society and technology has changed all that. We confront threats to privacy undreamed of 200 years ago. Private conversations are often conducted by telephone. Many personal records are held by institutions, such as banks and government agencies, and the Supreme Court has held that the individual has no constitutional rights over such records. Important judgments about people—such as the decision to extend credit or write an insurance policy—are often made by strangers, on the basis of recorded data.

New threats to privacy

Whenever we take out a loan, apply for insurance, receive treatment at a hospital, obtain government assistance, or pay

---

[22] *Weekly Compilation of Presidential Documents.* Administration of Jimmy Carter, presidential documents, week ending Friday, April 6, 1979. Monday, April 9, 1979, Vol. 15, No. 14, pp. 581–587.

our taxes, we add to the store of recorded information about our lives. That store is growing exponentially: in 1940, for example, 1.2 billion checks were written—in 1970 it was 7.2 billion. Personal information on millions of Americans is being flashed across the nation from computer to computer.

These changes are not the product of any plan to invade our privacy. They have developed naturally with the growth of our economy, the expansion of public and private institutions, the mobility of our citizens and the invention of computers and telecommunications systems.

Modern information systems are essential to our economy. They contribute to the comfort and convenience of our lives. But they can be misused to create a dangerously intrusive society.

Our challenge is to provide privacy safeguards that respond to these social changes without disrupting the essential flow of information.

Much has already been done. Laws are in place to restrict wiretapping. Last year Congress strengthened those protections by legislating restrictions on national security wiretaps. The Privacy Act of 1974 set rules for Federal agencies' record keeping. The Fair Credit Reporting Act and related Acts gave consumers the right to know information about themselves contained in the records of credit-reporting bureaus. The Family Educational Rights and Privacy Act gave students the right to see personal records held by educational institutions. Last year, the Congress passed the Financial Privacy Act, placing controls on Federal agencies' access to bank records.

These protections are a good beginning, but they were adopted piecemeal and have limited scope. It is time to establish a broad, national privacy policy to protect individual rights in the information age, as recommended by the Privacy Protection Study Commission.

I propose a privacy policy based on two principles:

• *Fair Information Practices.* Standards must be provided for handling sensitive, personal records. Individuals should be told what kind of information is being collected about them, how it will be used, and to whom it will be disclosed. They should be able to see and obtain a copy of the records and correct any errors. They should be told the basis for an adverse decision that may be based on personal data. And they should be able to prevent improper access to the records.

• *Limits on the Government.* Government access to and use of personal information must be limited and supervised so that power over information cannot be used to threaten our liberties.

The policy I am proposing will not disrupt the flow of information needed for legitimate business operations. Businesses

Natural growth of recordkeeping systems

Information systems are a double-edged sword

Prior legislation

Proposed privacy policy

gain by establishing good record-keeping systems and by keeping the trust of their customers and employees.

Nor will this policy prevent government agencies from collecting the information they need to enforce the laws. It will strengthen, not impede, the ability of reporters to cover the news. It will not impose heavy costs, and it will not create any new regulatory structures. Instead, it will establish a framework for private and government activity to prevent privacy abuses.

Responsibility for implementing policy

The responsibility for implementing this policy should be shared by the Federal government, by state and local governments, and by private institutions. I propose that the Federal government concentrate on improving its own activities and on setting standards for non-Federal record systems that contain particularly sensitive data and either involve Federal funding or require nationwide, uniform rules. We are submitting three bills to Congress today to address these areas, and a fourth major proposal will follow soon.

Base for state and local governments

State and local governments should build on this base to ensure that their own record systems are properly protected. In addition, a key element of the policy I am proposing is voluntary action by private businesses and organizations.

I. Fair Information Practices

To establish privacy safeguards for key record systems, I have these proposals:

Medical Records

Privacy of Medical Information Act

The "Privacy of Medical Information Act" is being submitted to you today. It establishes privacy protections for information maintained by almost all medical institutions. The Act will give individuals the right to see their own medical records. If direct access may harm the patient, the Act provides that access may be provided through an intermediary. This legislation allows the individual to ensure that the information maintained as part of his medical care relationship is accurate, timely, and relevant to that care. Such accuracy is of increasing importance because medical information is used to affect employment and collection of insurance and other social benefits.

The Act also limits the disclosure of medical information, and makes it illegal to collect medical information under false pretenses. The legislation allows disclosure when it is needed for medical care and other legitimate purposes, such as verifying insurance claims, and for research and epidemiological studies. In such cases, redisclosure is restricted.

FINANCIAL RECORDS

The Administration will soon submit the "Fair Financial Information Practices Act." This bill will expand the laws on consumer credit and banking records to provide full fair information protections. It will ensure that consumers are informed about firms' record keeping practices and thereby help them decide which firm to patronize. Specific requirements will be tailored to fit the varying information practices of the industries.

Fair Financial Information Practices Act

The bill will also provide, for the first time, national privacy standards for insurance records. This is a major step forward into an area where individuals have few such protections. The bill is not intended to change the existing pattern of regulating insurance at the state level, and it allows state regulators to oversee compliance. However, it will minimize the danger that a welter of differing state privacy standards will confuse the public and impose heavy costs on the insurance industry.

In addition, this bill will restrict disclosure of data from electronic funds transfer (EFT) systems. Although the emergence of EFT is relatively recent, its potential impact on our lives is enormous. Americans are benefitting from EFT in a variety of ways: automatic deposit of a paycheck in a bank account; automatic payment of a mortgage installment; cash dispensing machines; and so on. EFT terminals have the potential to supplant cash, checks and credit cards in a broad range of consumer transactions, from supermarket purchases to auto rentals. Such systems are efficient, but they pose major privacy problems. Not only do they contain extensive personal data on individuals, but they can be used to keep track of people's movements and activities. This legislation will erect safeguards against misuse of these systems while allowing flexibility for commercial and technological innovation.

Applicability to electronic funds transfer

RESEARCH RECORDS

Federally-supported research collection is vital for improved medical care, for cost-effective regulations, for economic analysis, and for many other purposes. In most cases, the information collected for these purposes is submitted voluntarily, is quite personal, and is collected on an express or implied pledge of confidentiality. That pledge is often essential to obtain individuals' cooperation in providing the information and ensuring its accuracy and completeness. However, in most cases there is no legal basis at present to guarantee the promise of confidentiality.

Privacy of Research Records Act

The "Privacy of Research Records Act" is being submitted today. This bill will ensure that personal information collected or maintained for a research purpose may not be used or disclosed in individually identifiable form for an action that adversely affects the individual.

We are also developing separate legislation to reduce the amount of information government collects in the first place through improved oversight and through carefully controlled sharing arrangements.

OTHER RECORD SYSTEMS

The Privacy Commission recommended against Federal legislation on employment records and proposed instead that employers be asked to establish voluntary policies to protect their employees' privacy. I agree.

Employment records

Many employers are already adopting the standards established by the Commission. Business groups, including the Business Roundtable, the Chamber of Commerce, and the National Association of Manufacturers, are encouraging such voluntary action. I urge other employers to take similar action, and I have instructed the Secretary of Labor to work with employer and employee groups in the implementation of these standards.

The Commission did urge one piece of legislation in the employment area—limits on the use of lie detectors in private employment. Such legislation already has been introduced in this Congress, and I urge you to proceed favorably with it.

Credit agencies

I also urge commercial credit grantors and reporting services to adopt voluntary fair information standards, to avoid any need for Federal legislation in this area.

It is critical that the privacy of those who receive public assistance and social services be adequately protected. I call upon the states to move forward with legislation to provide such protections, consistent with the Privacy Commission's recommendations and the need to prevent fraud in these programs. I have instructed the Secretary of Health, Education and Welfare to develop minimum privacy standards for these Federally funded programs.

Public assistance and social services

I also urge the states to act on other state and local record systems, particularly those of criminal justice agencies.

II. FEDERAL GOVERNMENT ACTIVITIES

I am also announcing measures to strengthen safeguards on Federal investigations and record-keeping.

Federal investigations

The bills on medical and financial records will ensure that the government obtains access to such records only for legitimate purposes. In most cases, the individual will be notified and given an opportunity to contest such access. I have these additional proposals:

GOVERNMENT ACCESS TO NEWS MEDIA FILES

The Supreme Court's decision last year in *Zurcher v. Stanford Daily* poses dangers to the effective functioning of our free press. I announced in December that we would develop legislation to protect First Amendment activities from unnecessarily intrusive searches while preserving legitimate law enforcement interests. Although regulations already restrict Federal officers' investigation of the news media, the problems raised by the *Stanford Daily* case require new, stringent safeguards against Federal, state and local governmental intrusion into First Amendment activities.

Free press

I am submitting this legislation today. It will restrict police searches for documentary materials held by the press and by others involved in the dissemination of information to the public. With limited exceptions, the bill will prohibit a search for or seizure of "work product"—such as notes, interview files and film. For documents which do not constitute work product, the bill requires that the police first obtain a subpoena rather than a search warrant. This ensures that police will not rummage through files of people preparing materials for publication and that those subject to the subpoena have the opportunity to contest the government's need for the information.

Police searches

WIRETAPPING

The privacy of personal communication is an important civil liberty. Americans are entitled to rely on that privacy, except where a legitimate and urgent law enforcement or national security purpose creates an overriding need. The fact that the person who is the target of surveillance is usually unaware of it argues for the tightest controls and for public accountability for the officials who authorize surveillance.

Personal communication

Title III of the Omnibus Crime Control and Safe Streets Act of 1968 governs the use of electronic surveillance of wire and oral communications except in matters involving foreign intelligence and counterintelligence. The National Commission for the Review of Federal and State Laws Relating to Wiretapping and Electronic Surveillance has studied the experience under Title III and has issued findings and recommendations.

I am transmitting to Congress today a letter which sets forth my detailed views concerning those recommendations. In general I endorse the recommended adjustments which would

Wiretaps

strengthen Title III's protections for individual privacy. I do not, however, support the recommendation to amend the law to allow Federal officials below the rank of Assistant Attorney General to apply to the courts for wiretaps. Such a change would diminish accountability and increase the danger of misuse. Also, I am not convinced that the list of criminal statutes for which electronic surveillance orders may be obtained should be expanded. I have asked the Attorney General to consult with the Secretary of the Treasury and with the Congress on those Commission recommendations.

FEDERAL RECORDS

Surveillance

The Federal Government holds almost four billion records on individuals, most of them stored in thousands of computers. Federally-funded projects have substantial additional files. This information is needed to run the social security system, collect taxes, conduct research, measure the economy, and for hundreds of other important purposes. Modern technology, however, makes it possible to turn this store into a dangerous surveillance system. Reasonable restrictions are needed on the collection and use of this information.

New data systems

The Privacy Act of 1974 established privacy safeguards for Federal records. It prevents agencies from collecting certain kinds of information, such as information about political beliefs; requires public notice whenever a new data system is established; gives individuals the right to see and correct their records; and limits disclosure of personal information.

While the Privacy Act is working reasonably well and is too new to decide on major revisions, I have ordered a number of administrative actions to improve its operation.

We are issuing today final guidelines for Federal agencies on the use of "matching programs." These programs compare computerized lists of individuals to detect fraud or other abuses. Such programs are making an important contribution to reducing abuse of Federal programs and are thereby saving taxpayers' money. However, safeguards are needed to protect the privacy of the innocent and to ensure that the use of "matching" is **Matching systems** properly limited. The guidelines, which were developed with public participation, will ensure that these programs are conducted:

- only after the public has been notified and given the opportunity to identify privacy problems;
- with tight safeguards on access to the data and on disclosure of the names of suspects identified by matching;

- only when there are no cost-effective, alternative means of identifying violators.

I have also directed that action be taken to:

- extend Privacy Act protections to certain data systems operated by recipients of Federal grants;
- strengthen administration of the "routine use" provision of the Privacy Act, which governs disclosures of personal information by Federal agencies;
- ensure that each Federal agency has an office responsible for privacy issues raised by the agency's activities;
- improve the selection and training of the system managers required by the Privacy Act;
- improve oversight of new Federal information systems at an early state in the planning process; and
- limit the amount of information the government requires private groups and individuals to report.

Federal agency recordkeeping

The Office of Management and Budget, as the unit responsible for overseeing Federal agency record-keeping, will implement these actions. I have assigned the Commerce Department's National Telecommunications and Information Administration to be the lead agency on other privacy matters and to work with Congress on the continuing development of privacy policy.

INTERNATIONAL PRIVACY ISSUES

The enormous increase in personal data records in the U.S. has been matched in other advanced countries. Throughout Western Europe, as well as in Canada, Australia, and Japan, records of personal data have grown at explosive rates. Our concerns about privacy are shared by many other governments.

International information flows, however, are increasingly important to the world's economy. We are, therefore, working with other governments in several international organizations to develop principles to protect personal data crossing international borders and to harmonize each country's rules to avoid needless disruption of international communications. Enactment of the proposals I have outlined will help speed this process by assuring other countries that the U.S. is committed to the protection of personal data.

International information flow

Privacy is a permanent public issue. Its preservation requires constant attention to social and technological changes, and those changes demand action now.

I ask the Congress and the public to join me in establishing a comprehensive framework of reasonable privacy protections. Together we can preserve the right to privacy in the information age.

JIMMY CARTER

The White House,
April 2, 1979.

OTHER COUNTRIES

This chapter has covered the data protection legislation and related activities of countries for which descriptive literature is readily available and for which the policies, procedures, and effective legislation can serve as a precedent to other nations. Clearly, the material in this chapter is not exhaustive, nor is it intended to be so. Table 5.1 gives other countries that are engaged in similar activity.

SUMMARY

Advances in computer and communications technology have occurred so rapidly that they have exceeded the ability of existing domestic and international institutions to cope with them. Because the level of international interdependence has increased substantially, a global information policy is needed. Several international organizations that have been active in this area include:

- Organization for Economic Cooperation and Development (OECD)
- Council of Europe
- UNESCO

Nations that have been heavily engaged in privacy and data protection legislation include:

- United States
- Austria
- Sweden
- Germany
- France
- Canada
- Brazil

Other countries are similarly involved.

Several international legislatures have considered—and some have enacted—privacy and/or data protection laws governing personal data, which could affect the design and operation of multinational computer systems. These laws encompass transborder data flow. Although on the surface the objective is to protect personal privacy through systems of licensing and registration, the underlying objectives in some cases are economic and political. The factors contributing to this legislative activity are reasonably well defined, and the legislative trends among various countries possess some degree of consistency. Overall, however, unilateral efforts can easily lead to a patchwork of laws that are mutually incompatible, which could inhibit the international flow of information.

Thus far, international organizations, such as those listed previously, have emphasized international participation in order to obtain a broad perspective on problems of freedom, privacy, and national sovereignty. Several international policy and working groups have been established.

Legislative activity in the areas of privacy and data regulation in Austria, Sweden, Germany, and France is ostensibly an effort to protect against the negative consequences of modern information technology. Concerns in Canada and Brazil have centered around economic issues.

In April 1979, President Carter submitted legislation to the Congress regarding medical, financial, and research records. The legislation is based on two principles: fair information practices and limits on the government. The president also announced strengthened safeguards concerning access to news media files, wiretapping, and matching systems.

IMPORTANT TERMS AND CONCEPTS

The reader should be familiar with the following terms and concepts:

Blocked data
Contractual relationship
Economy of scale
Electronic data banks
Enforcement
Erasure
Fair information practice
Indirect benefits of data regulation

Licensing
Manual data banks
Monitoring
Negative consequences of modern information technology
Official notification
Omnibus laws
Picket fence legislation
Punitive measures
Right of access
Verification

READINGS AND REFERENCES

Data Regulation: European and Third World Realities, Proceedings of the Online Conference, New York, November 1978.

Eger, J. M. The Brussels Mandate: An Alliance for the Future of World Communications and Information Policy. Address before the Conference on Transnational Data Regulation, Brussels, Belgium, February 9, 1978.

The London Meeting of the Brussels Mandate: Summary Report and Findings, June 15–16, 1978, London. Available from: The Brussels Mandate, 1742 N Street, N.W., Washington, D.C., 20036.

Marks, H. E., Crossborder data nets become targets of European lawmakers. *Data Communications* (September 1978), pp. 67–76.

Pipe, G. R. Three nations to pass privacy laws in '79, more may follow suit. *Computerworld* (February 12, 1979), p. 20.

Transnational Data Regulation. Proceedings of the Online Conference, Brussels, February 1978.

6
MULTINATIONAL SYSTEMS

It can be argued that the largest single causal factor operating on society today (by a very long way) is science, scientific application and technology, and we have a lot to learn about the effect which these causal factors have had on society already and will have in the future.

F. H. GEORGE

It is evident from the preceding chapters that we exist in a competitive society in which economies are largely intertwined. The situation is not one of survival, but rather of the development, preservation, and analysis of social values. The fundamental processes of society are monitoring and evaluation, and these can be expected to continue as long as social advances are being made in modern society. The danger of myopia is ever present, however, and one is constantly aware of the possibility of "not seeing the forest for the trees" and "winning the battle and losing the war."

Monitoring and evaluation of social values

The subject of course is information technology, and the question is, Where is it going? In the present context, technology is a "tool" of society—not an end in itself, but rather a developmental process in which benefits and costs are balanced in an economic sense. The forces of science and technology are important causal factors in our society and are the basis of much quasi-political activity. In reviewing the literature on transnational data regulation, the notion of "stabilizing the effects of the information revolution" frequently surfaces. While the concepts of science and technology may be universal, the effects are definitely not the same everywhere. It would seem that the regulation of information technology—i.e., bringing it under the scope of international law—is particularly inappropriate at this time. This

Technology is an important causal force

The regulation of information technology is inappropriate at this time

93

is especially true because we do not actually have knowledge of the totality of benefits to society that is inherent in the escalating advances in computer and communications technology.

ECONOMICS AND INFORMATION

A major product of the era of computers and communications technology is information, which is changing the nature of work, business, and recreation.* It has been estimated that 70 percent of the direct and indirect costs of business involve the collection, distribution, and management of information.[1] Speed and accuracy of information processing are necessary to support the complexities of national and international businesses, such that we are dependent upon computers and communications to support day-to-day business operations. Exchange rates, commodity prices, and schedules fluctuate rapidly, and ordinary business transactions, such as bids, transfers, and credits, are commonly handled in less than a day. In fact, international banking, airlines, and data base services are totally reliant on modern information technology.

International business is dependent upon computers and communications to sustain day-to-day operations

One concept with which participatory nations are concerned is the notion of information as an international resource—an economic good subject to considerations of the marketplace, pricing, and economies of scale—that can be exported and imported. While information per se is not a taxable commodity vis-á-vis transborder data flow, information and computational services are marketable items. In fact, three basic marketing functions of manufacturing, distribution, and retail services presently exist:

Information is an international resource

Services are a marketable item

- *Manufacturing:* producers of data bases accessible via computers and communications

Marketing functions

- *Distribution:* companies that maintain large computer-based information systems that provide wholesale dissemination of information and associated computer and communications facilities

- *Retail services:* local service companies that provide informational services based on the amount of information accessed

* One of the most promising definitions of information is that it is the change in knowledge over time: $I = dk/dt$.

[1] Pipe, G. R. Transnational data regulations. *Information Technology News* (1979), Horizon House, p. 1.

Already, informational services, such as Viewdata, are available in Europe as household commodities. Serious consideration is being given in some circles to charging for the amount of information carried on a communications circuit and not solely for the time that the circuit is used.

STRUCTURE OF INFORMATION ECONOMY

The interrelationships among questions of national sovereignty, privacy, human rights, and informational and computational services have yet to be established. Nevertheless, it has been suggested that an analysis of the situation can be resolved through an identification of the four levels of structure in an information economy.[2]

Four levels of structure exist

The first level is an *infrastructure,* designed to carry raw data without associated meaning. The infrastructure constitutes the medium of communications and includes facilities such as satellites, networks, switches, communications channels, and associated protocols and procedures. The infrastructure essentially involves the mechanisms necessary to move data.

Infrastructure

The *value-added processes* of storing and forwarding messages is the next level in the information economy. It involves the storage and computational elements necessary to support the logical and decisionmaking activities of a computer and communications network.

Value-added processes

The third level involves *computational, data processing,* and *data base activity*. At this level, meaning is given to data, resulting in information or the rate of change of knowledge, as mentioned previously. It necessarily follows that considerations of ownership, privacy, information economics, and informational transactions occur at this level. In addition, data regulatory activity is normally aimed at this level.

Computer activity

The last level in the structure of an information economy is the *message,* which is the ethical and social value attached to a unit of information by a societal group. Most nations prefer to have some degree of control and censorship over incoming messages.

The message

As we proceed upward in the structure from infrastructure to messages, both the desirability and feasibility of international agreements seem to diminish. Not only is national

Issues become cloudy

[2] The London Meeting of the Brussels Mandate: Summary Report and Findings, June 15–16, 1978, London, p. 11. Available from The Brussels Mandate, 1742 N Street, N. W., Washington, D.C. 20036.

sovereignty of concern here, but the issues also become cloudy enough to limit visibility.

POLICY ANALYSIS AND DECISIONMAKING

Welfare of the citizens

Most societies use private and public methods of policy analysis and decisionmaking to promote the welfare of its citizens. Public choices are performed by government decisionmakers through policies and laws. Private choices are made through the market system as a whole. In light of the two avenues for choice, an important question is, why regulate at all?

Governments regulate to achieve desirable outcomes, especially when one or more of the following events have occurred:

When governments regulate

- The market system has failed through a lack of competition.
- The predicted end state of existing competition is undesirable.
- The market process is unattractive because of the competitive behavior and ethical consequences it fosters.

Justification for regulation

Thus, regulation is generally justified for two basic reasons: (1) equity in the distribution of goods and services and (2) greater market efficiency.

Information is a resource and a commodity

A key ingredient in an effective market system is information—both as a resource and a commodity. In order for the market system to function in either case, information must be readily available, and the nature of services must be understood.

Which method of policy analysis and decisionmaking should we use?

In the case of information technology, the issues are sufficiently complex to severely limit the visibility of the decisionmaker. Will data protection legislation create barriers to trade in both information services and other commodities? Will current trends result in restrictive policies on the export of space-age technology further down the road? Clearly, these are rhetorical questions. The key question is whether we are in a position to apply the commonly used technique of synoptic policy analysis to the regulation of computer and communications technology. (Methods of policy analysis are summarized in Table 6–1.) Since this method, along with less powerful methods, involves the identification of alternatives

Table 6-1. Strategies of Political Decision. [a]

Naive conceptions is the naive criteria method wherein a few general values are used for policy evaluation and decisionmaking. (In the present context, representative values might be personal privacy and protectionism.) This method may be extended by prioritizing the values in some kind of preference ranking.

Rational deduction involves the synthesis of a set of principles through rational methods of analysis. Evaluation proceeds by applying the principles to an alternative and thereby determining its relative merits.

Welfare function involves the identification of features of each state of society that are subject to preference. Rules for the manipulation of numerical utilities are established, and the resultant values are used to form a general impression of a state of society.

Synoptic policy analysis involves the development of an exhaustive set of alternatives that are carefully analyzed with all of their possible consequences. The various consequences are then evaluated using the decisionmaker's value structure.

Disjointed incrementalism involves a concentration on margins or increments of one possible policy decision over another. Commonly used when future states of society are impossible to identify and difficult to evaluate, disjointed incrementalism concentrates on the incremental alteration of social states. Only policies are considered whose expected social states will differ incrementally from other recognized states and decisionmaking entails the ranking, by order of preference, of the increments by which social states differ.

[a] This table is a brief summarization of the methods contained in Braybrooke, D. and C. E. Lindblom. *A Strategy of Decision: Policy Evaluation as a Social Process.* New York: The Free Press, 1970.

and the evaluation of all possible future states before policy analysis and decisionmaking, a less comprehensive approach seems to be in order. Broad, sweeping legislation based on "possible" future states and a corresponding estimate of social welfare could probably result in undesirable consequences due to the rapid pace of technological innovation in the fields of computers and communications.

The synoptic and social welfare methods are inappropriate

It follows that a more realistic method of policy analysis and decisionmaking would be the method of "disjointed incrementalism." Many analysts prefer this method because unattainable social states need not be evaluated and corrective action can be taken before permanent damage is done. The method is summarized by Braybrooke and Lindblom:

A realistic method of policy analysis is disjointed incrementalism

Seen this way, the concept of problem solving by the strategy is this: The analyst makes an incremental move in the desired direction without taking upon himself the difficulties of finding

This method effectively reduces the task of analysis

a solution. He disregards many other possible moves because they are too costly (in time, energy, or money) to examine. For the move he makes, he does not trouble to find out (again, because it is too costly to do so) what all its consequences are. If his move fails or is attended by unanticipated adverse consequences, he assumes that someone's (perhaps even his own) next move will take care of the resulting problem. If his policy-making is remedial and serial, his assumptions are usually correct. . . . The process we have outlined for the strategy does not, therefore, successively approximate any "solution" but continues to change with changing values and policy possibilities.[3]

The difference between the synoptic and incremental approaches is analogous to the difference in mathematics between exact computation and successive approximation.

BOUNDED RATIONALITY

The incremental method of policy analysis and decision-making is similar in scope and concept to the notion of "bounded rationality" recognized by Nobel laureate Herbert Simon in his 1947 study of administrative organizations.

Rationality is bounded by practical considerations

Simon claimed that perfect rationality does not correspond to real-world decisionmaking; in essence, rationality is "bounded" because of practical considerations:

Rationality requires a complete knowledge and anticipation of the consequences that will follow on each choice. . . .In fact, knowledge of consequences is always fragmentary. Since these consequences lie in the future, imagination must supply the lack. . . .Rationality requires a choice among all possible alternative behaviors. In actual behavior, only a very few of all these possible alternatives come to mind.[4]

In fact, Simon continues, the concept applies to organizations in general:

It is now clear that the elaborate organizations that human beings have constructed in the modern world to carry out the work of production and government can only be understood as

---

[3] Braybrooke, D. and C. E. Lindblom. *A Strategy of Decision: Policy Evaluation as a Social Process* pp. 123–124. New York: The Free Press, 1970.
[4] Herbert Simon's economics, *Mosaic* (May/June 1979), p. 33.

machinery for coping with the limits of man's abilities to comprehend and compute in the face of complexity and uncertainty.[5]

Although bounded rationality has been viewed as "muddling through," it is significant because it recognizes the practicalities of the real world and the complexities of policy analysis and decisionmaking.

"Muddling through"

SOCIETAL BENEFITS OF MULTINATIONAL SYSTEMS

Transnational data flow is relevant to multinational computer systems in four instances:

1. Data service companies that provide processing and data base facilities on a national and international basis.
2. On-line computer systems of multinational organizations, wherein access to computer facilities can be made from a remote location.
3. International computer networks for airline reservations and interbank transfer.
4. Distributed data processing and distributed data base systems of multinational organizations. (See pp. 34–36.)

Scope of multinational computer systems

Individuals and organizations engaged in multinational computer systems activity believe that the premature stabilization of the opportunity for transnational data flow will result in a loss of important societal benefits. William C. Norris, founder, chairman, and president of the Control Data Corp., a multinational leader in computing and financial services, has identified and listed several of the societal benefits of transborder data flow:

William C. Norris

- Education—replacement of the present labor-intensive process with a capital-intensive productive technology.
- Health—widespread availability of automated health care, disease control, and medical treatment systems.
- Weather—observation, collection, and distribution of weather information in a timely and reliable manner.

Societal benefits of transborder data flow

[5] Ibid., p. 34.

- Food—understanding of climatic conditions and the application of advanced technology to food delivery systems.
- Technology transfer—reduced replication of technological effort and access to libraries and laboratory information.
- Job creation—increased employment resulting from economic growth inherent in advanced technology and informational efficiency.[6]

Benefits to LDCs

Moreover, several participants in the transnational data flow issue believe that the lesser developed countries would benefit most from the advanced technology associated with computers and communications.

United States dependence

There is an underlying fear among certain European groups that continued activity vis-á-vis transnational data flow will create a dependence upon the United States because of the widespread availability of information services. Clearly, this is not entirely the case, and a quote from a recent publication serves to squelch any debate on the issue:

France has the largest service companies in Europe

The French government reasoned that as the cost of data processing was going to fall so dramatically, one of the best sectors to be in would be the higher value added area of services. The extent to which the French seem to have got a hold of this activity in Europe is well demonstrated in the recent Quantum Sciences/European Computing Services Association survey. This shows that France has far and away the largest services companies in Europe, and also accounts for a large proportion of European business. Seven nations are represented in Europe's Top Thirty list for 1977. Adding together the combined European business of these different service companies, the ranking list by country comes out like this:

France: $566 million
US: $423 million (including IBM and Control Data). Estimates including Honeywell bring the total to $493 million
Germany: $116 million
Denmark: $99 million
Sweden: $74 million
UK: $73 million
Holland: $21 million

At the time of the ECSA survey, France accounted for almost one quarter of the European market for data processing services, another incentive for home grown service companies.

[6] Norris, W. C. A businessman's perspective on the transborder data flow issue, pp. 1–11. In *Data Regulation: European and Third World Realities.* Uxbridge, England: Online Conferences, Ltd., 1978.

What is more significant is that France's industry has continued to grow, and the big companies have grown faster than the small ones, since the survey.[7]

The revenue inherent in the preceding data supports the development of domestic computer services and data bases. However, development costs are high, and technical resources, including personnel, may not be available locally. The cost of regulation itself may be prohibitive. There are other considerations too. Certain types of information may only be available in foreign data banks, and routine data processing and information services may be less expensive through economy of scale.

Costs of developing domestic computer services and data bases

Thus, a nation desiring to develop a domestic computer and communications capability has two general policy options:

1. Restrict the flow of information in some manner in order to protect the local service.
2. Allow transnational data flow to take place but subsidize the local information industry to artificially create a competitive situation.

Policy options for a domestic computer and communications capability

In the latter case, services would be available at the lowest possible rate, but a national expenditure would be necessary to sustain the local service companies until they were self-sufficient. Once established, however, a domestic information service industry could have difficulty marketing its services to foreign countries.

DISTRIBUTED SYSTEMS

A *distributed system* is one in which computers are located at sites that are remote from a central computing facility. These computers possess the physical attributes that allow them to function as stand-alone data processing systems, to interact with the central facility, and possibly to interact with each other. The objective of a distributed system is to process information where it is most effective to satisfy operational, economic, or geographic conditions. A distributed system may also be characterized by a local data store for files and data bases. In a distributed system, programs and data may

The objective of a distributed system is to store and process information where it is most effective

[7] Lloyd, A. Stress on services in France. *Systems International* (June 1979), p. 13.

be transferred between adjacent sites. Therefore, some processing and informational requests can take place locally at the point of user activity, while other tasks can be dispersed in the network of computers.

Local options are available with distributed systems

Thus, through the use of a computer network, distributed data processing, and distributed data bases, an organization has the ability to store information wherever necessary in order to satisfy internal security, performance, and economic requirements. Privacy measures can be implemented locally without compromising the computational and informational viability of a multinational organization. Through advanced technological developments, we have literally "taken the computer to the work" rather than "the work to the computer."

We have "taken the computer to the work"

Distributed systems exist through the combination of microcomputers, minicomputers and advanced communications functions. Developments have been rapid, and the pace is not expected to decrease. While both hardware and communications costs are decreasing, hardware costs are decreasing more rapidly. As a result, machines will propagate. Any nation that isolates itself from expanded information processing through data regulation diminishes its capabilities for political, economic, and social growth.

Isolation can have negative consequences

SUMMARY

In a competitive society where economies are largely interrelated, constant concern surrounds social values and the ongoing processes of monitoring and evaluation.

The stabilization of computer and communications technology, with the possible threat that prohibitive legislation, can isolate a nation from the mainstream of world development.

Seventy percent of the direct and indirect costs of business involves the collection, distribution, and management of information. Moreover, national and international business are so complex that the speed and accuracy of computers and communications are necessary for sustaining day-to-day operations. Thus, information is both a resource and a commodity. A basic set of marketing functions for informational services exists, as does a structure for an information economy, which is outlined as follows:

- Infrastructure
- Value-added processes

- Computational, data processing, and data base activity
- Messages

In the area of multinational computer systems, policy analysis is complex because it is difficult to predict the end state of modern technology. One particularly appropriate method of analysis is disjointed incrementalism. In this context, we are dealing with "bounded rationality," as recognized by Nobel laureate Herbert Simon.

Transnational data flow relates to multinational computer systems in four instances:

- International service companies
- On-line systems of multinational organizations
- International service networks
- Distributed systems

The premature stabilization of transnational data flow can result in the loss of important societal benefits. Several benefits are listed, and those that would benefit most from the technology are the lesser developed countries.

Although the United States has created a substantial market for data services, the predominant data service country is France. However, the cost of development of domestic computer and communications capability is high, and the host country may have to resort to either of two policy options.

Recent advances related to multinational systems incorporate distributed data processing, distributed data bases, and computer networks. Through distributed systems, several worthwhile local options are available.

CONCLUSIONS

It is becoming increasingly apparent that much of the activity in the area of data regulation has its foundations in various economic and political issues ameliorated with concerns over personal privacy, data protection, and national security. Without duly considering the cost of replacement for goods and services related to computers and communications, some countries have used the concept of data regulation as an attractive opportunity to establish a domestic data processing capability. The reasons for this approach are varied and diverse, and normally include the fear of loss of control over information and the threat of increased dependency.

The creation of barriers to the free flow of information, however, may have severe economic repercussions to the parties involved. Even the costs of regulation and compliance are substantial. Monitoring and control are cumbersome, and many organizations are concerned over the disclosure of a company's activities to government.

Nevertheless, many governments believe data regulation to be a new challenge and a new responsibility. Without a doubt, privacy legislation is of prime importance. However, the use of data protection for economic and political purposes without due consideration of the consequences is particularly inappropriate in light of the rate of recent advances in information technology. Since the end state of current trends in computers and communications cannot be reliably predicted, broad sweeping legislation is likely to have negative consequences. An incremental approach to policy analysis and decisionmaking would seem more commensurate with the needs of the computer and communications community.

Multinational organizations and informational service companies are understandably concerned over certain aspects of data regulation since a predictable environment is needed for successful business operations. A key point is that protective legislation may backfire on countries desiring to expand domestic data services into the international arena.

IMPORTANT TERMS AND CONCEPTS

The reader should be familiar with the following terms and concepts:

Bounded rationality
Computation, data processing, and data base activity
Disjointed incrementalism
Distributed data base
Distributed system
Information (definition of)
Infrastructure
Market system
Message
Naive conceptions
Societal benefits
Synoptic policy analysis
Value-added processes
Welfare function

READINGS AND REFERENCES

Braybrooke, D. and C. E. Lindblom. *A Strategy of Decision: Policy Evaluation as a Social Process.* New York: The Free Press, 1970.

Castle, J. Network information services: the essential international business tool. In *Transnational Data Regulation: The Realities,* pp. 29-32. Uxbridge, England: On-line Conferences Ltd., 1979.

Chamoux, J. The networks development in Europe: practical and legal issues in 1978. In *Data Regulation: European and Third World Realities,* pp. 27-36. Uxbridge, England: Online Conferences Ltd., 1978.

Data Regulation: European and Third World Realities. Uxbridge, England: Online Conferences Ltd., 1978.

DeMaio, H. B. Transnational information flow: a perspective. In *Data Regulation: European and Third World Realities,* pp. 169-175. Uxbridge, England: Online Conferences Ltd., 1978.

Herbert Simon's Economics. *Mosaic* (May/June 1979), pp. 33-38.

Katzan, H. *Introduction to Distributed Data Processing,* Princeton, New Jersey: PBI-Petrocelli Books, 1979.

Lloyd, A. Stress on services in France. *Systems International* (June 1979), p. 13.

Norris, W. C. A businessman's perspective on the transborder data flow issue. In *Data Regulation: European and Third World Realities,* pp. 1-11. Uxbridge, England: Online Conferences Ltd., 1978.

Ohlin, T. The power of local information. *Telecommunications Policy* (September 1978), vol. 2, no. 3, pp. 234-243.

Pipe, G. R. Transnational data regulation. *Information Technology News* (1979), Horizon House, p. 1.

Safirstein, P. How do we best control the flow of electronic information across sovereign borders? *Proceedings of the 1979 National Computer Conference,* AFIPS, vol. 48, pp. 279-282.

Simon, H. A. *Administrative Behavior: A Study of Decision-Making Processes in Administrative Organization,* New York: The Free Press, 1957.

Stokey, E. and R. Zeckhauser. *A Primer for Policy Analysis.* New York: W. W. Norton and Company, Inc., 1978.

The London Meeting of The Brussels Mandate: Summary Report and Findings. London, June 15-16, 1978. (Available from the Brussels Mandate, 1742 N Street, NW, Washington, DC 20036.)

Turn, R. Implementation of privacy and security requirements in transnational data processing systems. In *Transnational Data Regulation: The Realities,* pp. 113-132. Uxbridge, England: Online Conferences Ltd., 1979.

Privacy and security in transnational data processing systems. *Proceedings of the 1979 National Computer Conference,* AFIPS, vol. 48, pp. 283-291.

Transnational Data Regulation. Uxbridge, England: Online Conferences, Ltd., 1978.

Zurkowski, P. G. The information industry and universal access. In *Data Regulation: European and Third World Realities,* pp. 207-213. Uxbridge, England: Online Conferences, Ltd., 1978.

Appendix A

SAFEGUARD REQUIREMENTS FOR ADMINISTRATIVE PERSONAL DATA SYSTEMS (Recommendations)*

I. GENERAL REQUIREMENTS

A. Any organization maintaining a record of individually identifiable personal data, which it does not maintain as part of an administrative automated personal data system, shall make no transfer of any such data to another organization, without the prior informed consent of the individual to whom the data pertain, if, as a consequence of the transfer, such data will become part of an administrative automated personal data system that is not subject to these safeguard requirements.

B. Any organization maintaining an administrative automated personal data system shall:

(1) Identify one person immediately responsible for the system, and make any other organizational arrangements

---

* U.S. Department of Health, Education, and Welfare. From *Records, Computers, and The Rights of Citizens.* Report of the Secretary's Advisory Committee on Automated Personal Data Systems. p. xxiv–xxvi. Cambridge, Massachusetts: M.I.T. Press, 1973.

that are necessary to assure continuing attention to the fulfillment of the safeguard requirements;

(2) Take affirmative action to inform each of its employees having any responsibility or function in the design, development, operation, or maintenance of the system, or the use of any data contained therein, about all the safeguard requirements and all the rules and procedures of the organization designed to assure compliance with them;

(3) Specify penalties to be applied to any employee who initiates or otherwise contributes to any disciplinary or other punitive action against any individual who brings to the attention of appropriate authorities, the press, or any member of the public, evidence of unfair information practice;

(4) Take reasonable precautions to protect data in the system from any anticipated threats or hazards to the security of the system;

(5) Make no transfer of individually identifiable personal data to another system without (i) specifying requirements for security of the data, including limitations on access thereto, and (ii) determining that the conditions of the transfer provide substantial assurance that those requirements and limitations will be observed—except in instances when an individual specifically requests that data about him be transferred to another system or organization;

(6) Maintain a complete and accurate record of every access to and use made of any data in the system, including the identity of all persons and organizations to which access has been given;

(7) Maintain data in the system with such accuracy, completeness, timeliness, and pertinence as is necessary to assure accuracy and fairness in any determination relating to an individual's qualifications, character, rights, opportunities, or benefits, that may be made on the basis of such data; and

(8) Eliminate data from computer-accessible files when the data are no longer timely.

II. PUBLIC NOTICE REQUIREMENT

Any organization maintaining an administrative automated personal data system shall give public notice of the existence and character of its system once each year. Any organization maintaining more than one system shall publish such annual notices for all its systems simultaneously. Any organization proposing to establish a new system, or to enlarge an existing system, shall give public notice long enough in advance of the initiation or enlargement of the system to assure individuals who may be affected by its operation a reasonable opportunity to comment. The public notice shall specify:

(1) The name of the system;

(2) The nature and purpose(s) of the system;

(3) The categories and number of persons on whom data are (to be) maintained;

(4) The categories of data (to be) maintained, indicating which categories are (to be) stored in computer-accessible files;

(5) The organization's policies and prctices regarding data storage, duration of retention of data, and disposal thereof;

(6) The categories of data sources;

(7) A description of all types of use (to be) made of data, indicating those involving computer-accessible files, and including all classes of users and the organizational relationships among them;

(8) The procedures whereby an individual can (i) be informed if he is the subject of data in the system; (ii) gain access to such data; and (iii) contest their accuracy, completeness, pertinence, and the necessity for retaining them;

(9) The title, name, and address of the person immediately responsible for the system.

III. RIGHTS OF INDIVIDUAL DATA SUBJECTS

Any organization maintaining an administrative automated personal data system shall:

(1) Inform an individual asked to supply personal data for the system whether he is legally required, or may refuse, to supply the data requested, and also of any specific consequences for him, which are known to the organization, of providing or not providing such data;

(2) Inform an individual, upon his request, whether he is the subject of data in the system, and, if so, make such data fully available to the individual, upon his request, in a form comprehensible to him;

(3) Assure that no use of individually identifiable data is made that is not within the stated purposes of the system as reasonably understood by the individual, unless the informed consent of the individual has been explicitly obtained;

(4) Inform an individual, upon his request, about the uses made of data about him, including the identity of all persons and organizations involved and their relationships with the system;

(5) Assure that no data about an individual are made available from the system in response to a demand for data made by means of compulsory legal process, unless the individual to whom the data pertain has been notified of the demand; and

(6) Maintain procedures that (i) allow an individual who is the subject of data in the system to contest their accuracy, completeness, pertinence, and the necessity for retaining them; (ii) permit data to be corrected or amended when the individual to whom they pertain so requests; and (iii) assure, when there is disagreement with the individual about whether a correction or amendment should be made, that the individual's claim is noted and included in any subsequent disclosure or dissemination of the disputed data.''

Appendix B

SAFEGUARD REQUIREMENTS FOR STATISTICAL-REPORTING AND RESEARCH SYSTEMS (Recommendations)*

I. GENERAL REQUIREMENTS

A. Any organization maintaining a record of personal data, which it does not maintain as part of an automated personal data system used exclusively for statistical reporting or research, shall make no transfer of any such data to another organization without the prior informed consent of the individual to whom the data pertain, if, as a consequence of the transfer, such data will become part of an automated personal data system that is not subject to these safeguard requirements or the safeguard requirements for administrative personal data systems.

B. Any organization maintaining an automated personal data system used exclusively for statistical reporting or research shall:

* U.S. Department of Health, Education and Welfare. *Records, Computers, and The Rights of Citizens.* Report of the Secretary's Advisory Committee on Automated Personal Data Systems, pp. xxix-xxxi. Cambridge, Massachusetts: M.I.T. Press, 1973.

(1) Identify one person immediately responsible for the system, and make any other organizational arrangements that are necessary to assure continuing attention to the fulfillment of the safeguard requirements;

(2) Take affirmative action to inform each of its employees having any responsibility or function in the design, development, operation, or maintenance of the system, or the use of any data contained therein, about all the safeguard requirements and all the rules and procedures of the organization designed to assure compliance with them;

(3) Specify penalties to be applied to any employee who initiates or otherwise contributes to any disciplinary or other punitive action against any individual who brings to the attention of appropriate authorities, the press, or any member of the public, evidence of unfair information practice;

(4) Take reasonable precautions to protect data in the system from any anticipated threats or hazards to the security of the system;

(5) Make no transfer of individually identifiable personal data to another system without (i) specifying requirements for security of the data, including limitations on access thereto, and (ii) determining that the conditions of the transfer provide substantial assurance that those requirements and limitations will be observed—except in instances when each of the individuals about whom data are to be transferred has given his prior informed consent to the transfer; and

(6) Have the capacity to make fully documented data readily available for independent analysis.

II. PUBLIC NOTICE REQUIREMENT

Any organization maintaining an automated personal data system used exclusively for statistical reporting or research shall give public notice of the existence and character of its system once each year. Any organization maintaining more than one such system shall publish annual notices for all its systems simultaneously. Any organization proposing to establish a new system or to enlarge an existing system, shall give public notice long enough in advance of the initiation or enlargement of the system to assure individuals who may be affected by its operation a reasonable opportunity to comment. The public notice shall specify:

(1) The name of the system;

(2) The nature and purpose(s) of the system;

(3) The categories and number of persons on whom data are (to be) maintained;

(4) The categories of data (to be) maintained, indicating which categories are (to be) stored in computer-accessible files;

(5) The organization's policies and practices regarding data storage, duration of retention of data, and disposal thereof;

(6) The categories of data sources;

(7) A description of all types of use (to be) made of data, indicating those involving computer-accessible files, and including all classes of users and the organizational relationships among them;

(8) The procedures whereby an individual, group, or organization can gain access to data for independent analysis;

(9) The title, name, and address of the person immediately responsible for the system;

(10) A statement of the system's provisions for data confidentiality and the legal basis for them.

III. RIGHTS OF INDIVIDUAL DATA SUBJECTS

Any organization maintaining an automated personal data system used exclusively for statistical reporting or research shall:

(1) Inform an individual asked to supply personal data for the system whether he is legally required, or may refuse, to supply the data requested, and also of any specific consequences for him, which are known to the organization, of providing or not providing such data;

(2) Assure that no use of individually identifiable data is made that is not within the stated purposes of the system as reasonably understood by the individual, unless the informed consent of the individual has been explicitly obtained;

(3) Assure that no data about an individual are made available from the system in response to a demand for data made by means of compulsory legal process, unless the individual to whom the data pertain (i) has been notified of the demand, and (ii) has been afforded full access to the data before they are made available in response to the demand.

Appendix C
PUBLIC LAW 93-579: PRIVACY ACT OF 1974

Be it enacted by the Senate and House of Representatives of the United States of America in Congress assembled, That this Act may be cited as the "Privacy Act of 1974."

Sec. 2.

(a) The Congress finds that—
   (1) the privacy of an individual is directly affected by the collection, maintenance, use, and dissemination of personal information by Federal agencies;
   (2) the increasing use of computers and sophisticated information technology, while essential to the efficient operations of the Government, has greatly magnified the harm to individual privacy that can occur from any collection, maintenance, use, or dissemination of personal information;
   (3) the opportunities for an individual to secure employment, insurance, and credit, and his right to due process, and other legal protections are endangered by the misuse of certain information systems;
   (4) the right to privacy is a personal and fundamental right protected by the Constitution of the United States; and
   (5) in order to protect the privacy of individuals identified in information systems maintained by Federal agencies, it is necessary and proper for the Congress to regulate the collection, maintenance, use, and dissemination of information by such agencies.
(b) The purpose of this Act is to provide certain safeguards for an individual against an invasion of personal privacy

by requiring Federal agencies, except as otherwise provided by law, to—

(1) permit an individual to determine what records pertaining to him are collected, maintained, used, or disseminated by such agencies;

(2) permit an individual to prevent records pertaining to him obtained by such agencies for a particular purpose from being used or made available for another purpose without his consent;

(3) permit an individual to gain access to information pertaining to him in Federal agency records, to have a copy made of all or any portion thereof, and to correct or amend such records;

(4) collect, maintain, use, or disseminate any record of identifiable personal information in a manner that assures that such action is for a necessary and lawful purpose, that the information is current and accurate for its intended use, and that adequate safeguards are provided to prevent misuse of such information;

(5) permit exemptions from the requirements with respect to records provided in this Act only in those cases where there is an important public policy need for such exemption as has been determined by specific statutory authority; and

(6) be subject to civil suit for any damages which occur as a result of willful or intentional action which violates any individual's rights under this Act.

Sec. 3.

Title 5, United States Code, is amended by adding after section 552 the following new section:

"552a. Records maintained on individuals

"(a) DEFINITIONS.-For purposes of this section—
    "(1) the term 'agency' means agency as defined in section 552(e) of this title;
    "(2) the term 'individual' means a citizen of the United States or an alien lawfully admitted for permanent residence;
    "(3) the term 'maintain' includes maintain, collect, use, or disseminate;
    "(4) the term "record' means any item, collection, or

grouping of information about an individual that is maintained by an agency, including, but not limited to, his education, financial transactions, medical history, and criminal or employment history and that contains his name, or the identifying number, symbol, or other identifying particular assigned to the individual, such as a finger or voice print or a photograph;

"(5) the term 'system of records' means a group of any records under the control of any agency from which information is retrieved by the name of the individual or by some identifying number, symbol, or other identifying particular assigned to the individual;

"(6) the term 'statistical record' means a record in a system of records maintained for statistical research or reporting purposes only and not used in whole or in part in making any determination about an identifiable individual, except as provided by section 8 of title 13; and

"(7) the term 'routine use' means, with respect to the disclosure of a record, the use of such record for a purpose which is compatible with the purpose for which it was collected.

"(b) CONDITIONS OF DISCLOSURE.-No agency shall disclose any record which is contained in a system of records by any means of communication to any person, or to another agency, except pursuant to a written request by, or with the prior consent of, the individual to whom the record pertains, unless disclosure of the record would be—

"(1) to those officers and employees of the agency which maintains the record who have a need for the record in the performance of their duties;

"(2) required under section 552 of this title;

"(3) for a routine use as defined in subsection (a)(7) of this section and described under subsection (e)(4) (D) of this section;

"(4) to the Bureau of the Census for purposes of planning or carrying out a census of survey or related activity pursuant to the provisions of title 13;

"(5) to a recipient who has provided the agency with advance adequate written assurance that the record will be used solely as a statistical research or reporting record, and the record is to be transferred in a form that is not individually identifiable;

"(6) to the National Archives of the United States as a record which has sufficient historical or other value to warrant its continued preservation by the United States Government, or for evaluation by the Administrator of General Services or his designee to determine whether the record has such value;

"(7) to another agency or to an instrumentality of any governmental jurisdiction whithin or under the control of the United States for a civil or criminal law enforcement activity if the activity is authorized by law, and if the head of the agency or instrumentality has made a written request to the agency which maintains the record specifying the particular portion desired and the law enforcement activity for which the record is sought;

"(8) to a person pursuant to a showing of compelling circumstances affecting the health or safety of an individual if upon such disclosure notification is transmitted to the last known address of such individual;

"(9) to either House of Congress, or, to the extent of matter within its jurisdiction, any committee or subcommittee thereof, any joint committee of Congress or subcommittee of any such joint committee;

"(10) to the Comptroller General, or any of his authorized representatives, in the course of the performance of the duties of the General Accounting Office; or

"(11) pursuant to the order of a court of competent jurisdiction.

"(c) ACCOUNTING OF CERTAIN DISCLOSURES— each agency, with respect to each system of records under its control, shall—

"(1) except for disclosures made under subsections (b)(1) or (b)(2) of this section, keep an accurate accounting of—

"(A) the date, nature, and purpose of each disclosure of a record to any person or to another agency made under subsection (b) of this section; and

"(B) the name and address of the person or agency to whom the disclosure is made;

"(2) retain the accounting made under paragraph (1) of this subsection for at least five years or the life of the record, whichever is longer, after the disclosure for which the accounting is made;

"(3) except for disclosures made under subsection (b)(7) of this section, make the accounting made under paragraph (1) of this subsection available to the individual named in the record at his request; and

"(4) inform any person or other agency about any correction or notation of dispute made by the agency in accordance with subsection (d) of this section of any record that has been disclosed to the person or agency if an accounting of the disclosure was made.

"(d) ACCESS TO RECORDS.—Each agency that maintains a system of records shall—

"(1) upon request by any individual to gain access to his record or to any information pertaining to him which is contained in the system, permit him and upon his request, a person of his own choosing to accompany him, to review the record and have a copy made of all or any portion thereof in a form comprehensible to him, except that the agency may require the individual to furnish a written statement authorizing discussion of that individual's record in the accompanying person's presence;

"(2) permit the individual to request amendment of a record pertaining to him and—

"(A) not later than 10 days (excluding Saturdays, Sundays, and legal public holidays) after the date of receipt of such request, acknowledge in writing such receipt; and

"(B) promptly, either—

"(i) make any correction of any portion thereof which the individual believes is not accurate, relevant, timely, or complete; or "(ii) inform the individual of its refusal to amend the record in accordance with his request, the reason for the refusal, the procedures established by the agency for the individual to request a review of that refusal by the head of the agency or an officer designated by the head of the agency, and the name and business address of that official;

"(3) permit the individual who disagrees with the refusal of the agency to amend his record to request a review of such refusal, and not later than 30 days (excluding Saturdays, Sundays, and legal public holidays) from the date on which the individual requests such review, complete such review and make a final determination unless, for good cause shown, the head of the agency extends such 30-day period; and if, after his review, the reviewing official also refuses to amend the record in accordance with the request, permit the individual to file with the agency a concise statement setting forth the reasons for his disagreement with the refusal of the agency, and notify the individual of the provisions for judicial review of the reviewing official's determination under subsection (g)(1)(A) of this section;

"(4) in any disclosure, containing information about which the individual has filed a statement of disagreement, occurring after the filing of the statement under paragraph (3) of this subsection, clearly note any portion of the record which is disputed and provide copies of the statement and, if the agency deems it appropriate, copies of a concise statement of the reasons of the agency for not making the amendments requested, to persons or other agencies to whom the disputed record has been disclosed; and

"(5) nothing in this section shall allow an individual access to any information compiled in reasonable anticipation of a civil action or proceeding.

"(e) AGENCY REQUIREMENTS.—Each agency that maintains a system of records shall—

"(1) maintain in its records only such information about an individual as is relevant and necessary to accomplish a purpose of the agency required to be accomplished by statute or by executive order of the President;

"(2) collect information to the greatest extent practicable directly from the subject individual when the information may result in adverse determinations about an individual's rights, benefits, and privileges under Federal programs;

"(3) inform each individual whom it asks to supply information, on the form which it uses to collect the information or on a separate form that can be retained by the individual—

"(A) the authority (whether granted by statute, or by executive order of the President) which authorizes the solicitation of the information and whether disclosure of such information is mandatory or voluntary;

"(B) the principal purpose or purposes for which the information is intended to be used;

"(C) the routine uses which may be made of the information, as published pursuant to paragraph (4)(D) of this subsection; and

"(D) the effects on him, if any, of not providing all or any part of the requested information;

"(4) subject to the provisions of paragraph (11) of this subsection, publish in the *Federal Register* at least annually a notice of the existence and character of the system of records, which notice shall include—

"(A) the name and location of the system;

"(B) the categories of individuals on whom records are maintained in the system;

"(C) the categories of records maintained in the system;

"(D) each routine use of the records contained in the system, including the categories of users and the purpose of such use;

"(E) the policies and practices of the agency regarding storage, retrievability, access controls, retention, and disposal of the records;

"(F) the title and business address of the agency official who is responsible for the system of records;

"(G) the agency procedures whereby an individual can be notified at his request if the system of records contains a record pertaining to him;

"(H) the agency procedures whereby an individual can be notified at his request how he can gain access to any record pertaining to him contained in the system of records, and how he can contest its content; and

"(I) the categories of sources of records in the system;

"(5) maintain all records which are used by the agency in making any determination about any individual with such accuracy, relevance, timeliness, and completeness as is reasonably necessary to assure fairness to the individual in the determination;

"(6) prior to disseminating any record about an individual to any person other than an agency, unless the dissemination is made pursuant to subsection (b)(2) of this section, make reasonable efforts to assure that such records are accurate, complete, timely, and relevant for agency purposes;

"(7) maintain no record describing how any individual exercises rights guaranteed by the First Amendment unless expressly authorized by statute or by the individual about whom the record is maintained or unless pertinent to and within the scope of an authorized law enforcement activity;

"(8) make reasonable efforts to serve notice on an individual when any record on such individual is made available to any person under compulsory legal process when such process becomes a matter of public record;

"(9) establish rules of conduct for persons involved in the design, development, operation, or maintenance of any system of records, or in maintaining any record, and instruct each such person with respect to such rules and the requirements of this section, including any other rules and procedures adopted pursuant to this section and the penalties for noncompliance;

"(10) establish appropriate administrative, technical,

and physical safeguards to insure the security and confidentiality of records and to protect against any anticipated threats or hazards to their security or integrity which could result in substantial harm, embarrassment, inconvenience, or unfairness to any individual on whom information is maintained; and

"(11) at least 30 days prior to publication of information under paragraph (4)(D) of this subsection, publish in the *Federal Register* notice of any new use or intended use of the information in the system, and provide an opportunity for interested persons to submit written data, views, or arguments to the agency.

"(f) AGENCY RULES.—In order to carry out the provisions of this section, each agency that maintains a system of records shall promulgate rules, in accordance with the requirements (including general notice) of section 553 of this title, which shall—

"(1) establish procedures whereby an individual can be notified in response to his request if any system of records named by the individual contains a record pertaining to him;

"(2) define reasonable times, places, and requirements for identifying an individual who requests his record or information pertaining to him before the agency shall make the record or information available to the individual;

"(3) establish procedures for the disclosure to an individual upon his request of his record or information pertaining to him, including special procedure, if deemed necessary, for the disclosure to an individual of medical records, including psychological records, pertaining to him;

"(4) establish procedures for reviewing a request from an individual concerning the amendment of any record or information pertaining to the individual, for making a determination on the request, for an appeal within the agency of an initial adverse agency determination, and for whatever additional means may be necessary for each individual to be able to exercise fully his rights under this section; and

"(5) establish fees to be charged, if any, to any individual for making copies of his record, excluding the cost of any search for and review of the record.

The Office of the Federal Register shall anually compile and publish the rules promulgated under this subsection and agency notices published under subsection (e)(4) of this section in a form available to the public at low cost.

"(g) —
  "(1) CIVIL REMEDIES.—Whenever any agency
    "(A) makes a determination under subsection (d)(3) of this section not to amend an individual's record in accordance with his request, or fails to make such review in conformity with that subsection;
    "(B) refuses to comply with an individual request under subsection (d)(1) of this section;
    "(C) fails to maintain any record concerning any individual with such accuracy, relevance, timeliness, and completeness as is necessary to assure fairness in any determination relating to the qualifications, character, rights, or opportunities of, or benefits to the individual that may be made on the basis of such record, and consequently a determination is made which is adverse to the individual; or
    "(D) fails to comply with any other provision of this section, or any rule promulgated thereunder, in such a way as to have an adverse effect on an individual,

the individual may bring a civil action against the agency, and the district courts of the United States shall have jurisdiction in the matters under the provisions of this subsection.

"(2) —
    "(A) In any suit brought under the provisions of subsection (g)(1)(A) of this section, the court may order the agency to amend the individual's record in accordance with his request or in such other way as the court may direct. In such a case the court shall determine the matter *de novo*.

"(B) The court may assess against the United States reasonable attorney fees and other litigation costs reasonably incurred in any case under this paragraph in which the complainant has substantially prevailed.

"(3) —

"(A) In any suit brought under the provisions of subsection (g)(1)(B) of this section, the court may enjoin the agency from withholding the records and order the production to the complainant of any agency records improperly withheld from him. In such a case the court shall determine the matter *de novo,* and may examine the contents of any agency records *in camera* to determine whether the records or any portion thereof may be withheld under any of the exemptions set forth in subsection (k) of this section, and the burden is on the agency to sustain its action.

"(B) The court may assess against the United States reasonable attorney fees and other litigation costs reasonably incurred in any case under this paragraph in which the complainant has substantially prevailed.

"(4) In any suit brought under the provisions of subsection (g)(1)(C) or (D) of this section in which the court determines that the agency acted in a manner which was intentional or willful, the United States shall be liable to the individual in an amount equal to the sum of—

"(A) actual damages sustained by the individual as a result of the refusal or failure, but in no case shall a person entitled to recovery receive less than the sum of $1,000; and

"(B) the costs of the action together with reasonable attorney fees as determined by the court.

"(5) An action to enforce any liability created under this section may be brought in the district court of the United States in the district in which the complainant resides, or has his principal place of business, or in which the agency records are situated, or in the District of Columbia, without regard to the amount in controversy, within two years from the date on which the cause of action arises, except that where any agency has materially and willfully misrepresented any information required under this section to be disclosed to an individual and the information so misrepresented is material to establishment of liability of the agency to the individual under this section, the action may be brought at any time within two years after discovery by the individual of the misrepresentation. Nothing in this section shall be construed to authorize any civil action by reason of any injury sustained as the result of a disclosure of a record prior to the effective date of this section.

"(h) RIGHTS OF LEGAL GUARDIANS.—For the purpose of this section, the parent of any minor, or the legal guardian of any individual who has been declared to be incompetent due to physical or mental incapacity or age by a court of competent jurisdiction, may act on behalf of the individual.

"(i) —

"(1) CRIMINAL PENALTIES.—Any officer or employee of an agency, who by virtue of his employment or official position, has possession of, or access to, agency records which contain individually identifiable information the disclosure of which is prohibited by this section or by rules or regulations established thereunder, and who knowing that disclosure of the specific material is so prohibited, willfully discloses the material in any manner to any person or agency not entitled to receive it, shall be guilty of a misdemeanor and fined not more than $5,000.

"(2) Any officer or employee of any agency who willfully maintains a system of records without meeting the notice requirements of subsection (e)(4) of this section shall be guilty of a misdemeanor and fined not more than $5,000.

"(3) Any person who knowingly and willfully requests or obtains any record concerning an individual from an agency under false pretenses be guilty of a misdemeanor and fined not more than $5,000.

"(j) GENERAL EXEMPTIONS.—The head of an agency may promulgate rules, in accordance with the requirements (including general notice) of sections 553(b)(1), (2), and (3), (c), and (e) of this title, to exempt any system of records within the agency from any part of this section except subsections (b), (c)(1) and (2), (e)(4)(A) through (F), (e)(6), (7), (9), (10), and (11), and (i) if the system of records is—

"(1) maintained by the Central Intelligence Agency; or

"(2) maintained by an agency or component thereof which performs as its principal function any activity pertaining to the enforcement of criminal laws, including police efforts to prevent, control, or reduce crime or to apprehend criminals, and the activities of prosecutors, courts, correctional, probation, pardon, or parole authorities, and which consists of (A) information compiled for the purpose of identifying individual criminal offenders and alleged offenders and consisting only of identifying data and notations of arrests, the nature and disposition of criminal charges, sentencing, confinement, release, and parole and probation status; (B) information compiled for the purpose of a criminal investigation, including reports of informants and investigators, and associated with an identifiable individual; or (C) reports identifiable to an individual compiled at any stage of the process of enforcement of criminal laws from arrest or indictment through release from supervision.

At the time rules are adopted under this subsection, the agency shall include in the statement required under section 553(c) of this title, the reasons why the system of records is to be exempted from a provision of this section.

"(k) SPECIFIC EXEMPTIONS.—The head of any agency may promulgate rules, in accordance with the requirements (including general notice) of sections 553(b)(1), (2), and (3), (c), and (e) of this title, to exempt any system of records within the agency from subsections (c)(3), (d), (e)(1), (e)(4)(G), (H), and (I) and (f) of this section if the system of records is—

"(1) subject to the provisions of section 552(b)(1) of this title;

"(2) investigatory material compiled for law enforcement purposes, other than material within the scope of subsection (j)(2) of this section: *Provided, however,* That if any individual is denied any right, privilege, or benefit that he would otherwise be entitled by Federal Law, or for which he would otherwise be eligible, as a result of the maintenance of such material, such material shall be provided to such individual, except to the extent that the disclosure of such material would reveal the identity of a source who furnished information to the Government under an express promise that the identity of the source would be held in confidence, or, prior to the effective date of this section, under an implied promise that the identity of the source would be held in confidence;

"(3) maintained in connection with providing protective services to the President of the United States or other individuals pursuant to Section 3056 of title 18;

"(4) required by statute to be maintained and used solely as statistical records;

"(5) investigatory material compiled solely for the purpose of determining suitability, eligibility, or qualifications for Federal civilian employment, military service, Federal contracts, or access to classified information, but only to the extent that the disclosure of such material would reveal the identity of a source who furnished information to the Government under an express promise that the identity of the source would be held in confidence, or, prior to the effective date of this section, under an implied promise that the identity of the source would be held in confidence;

"(6) testing or examination material used solely to determine individual qualifications for appointment or promotion in the Federal service the disclosure of which would compromise the objectivity or fairness of the testing or examination process; or

"(7) evaluation material used to determine potential for promotion in the armed services, but only to the extent that the disclosure of such material would reveal the identity of a source who furnished information to the Government under an

express promise that the identity of the source
would be held in confidence, or, prior to the effective date of this section, under an implied promise that the identity of the source would be held
in confidence.

At the time rules are adopted under this subsection,
the agency shall include in the statement required
under section 553(c) of this title, the reasons why the
system of records is to be exempted from a provision
of this section.

"(l) ARCHIVAL RECORDS.—

"(1) Each agency record which is accepted by the Administrator of General Services for storage, processing, and servicing in accordance with section
3103 of title 44 shall, for the purposes of this
section, be considered to be maintained by the
agency which deposited the record and shall be
subject to the provisions of this section. The Administrator of General Services shall not disclose
the record except to the agency which maintains
the record, or under rules established by that
agency which are not inconsistent with the provisions of this section.

"(2) Each agency record pertaining to an identifiable
individual which was transferred to the National
Archives of the United States as a record which
has sufficient historical or other value to warrant
its continued preservation by the United States
Government, prior to the effective date of this
section, shall, for the purposes of this section, be
considered to be maintained by the National Archives and shall not be subject to the provisions
of this section, except that a statement generally
describing such records (modeled after the requirements relating to records subject to subsections (e)(4)(A) through (G) of this section) shall
be published in the *Federal Register*.

"(3) Each agency record pertaining to an identifiable
individual which is transferred to the National
Archives of the United States as a record which
has sufficient historical or other value to warrant
its continued preservation by the United States
Government, on or after the effective date of this

section, shall, for the purposes of this section be considered to be maintained by the National Archives and shall be exempt from the requirements of this section except subsections (e)(4)(A) through (G) and (e)(9) of this section.

"(m) GOVERNMENT CONTRACTORS.—When an agency provides by a contract for the operation by or on behalf of the agency of a system of records to accomplish an agency function, the agency shall, consistent with its authority, cause the requirements of this section to be applied to such system. For purposes of subsection (i) of this section any such contractor and any employee of such contractor, if such contract is agreed to on or after the effective date of this section, shall be considered to be an employee of an agency.

"(n) MAILING LISTS.—An individual's name and address may not be sold or rented by an agency unless such action is specifically authorized by law. This provision shall not be construed to require the withholding of names and addresses otherwise permitted to be made public.

"(o) REPORT ON NEW SYSTEMS.—Each agency shall provide adequate advance notice to Congress and the Office of Management and Budget of any proposal to establish or alter any system of records in order to permit an evaluation of the probable or potential effect of such proposal on the privacy and other personal or property rights of individuals or the disclosure of information relating to such individuals, and its effect on the preservation of the constitutional principles of federalism and separation of powers.

"(p) ANNUAL REPORT.—The President shall submit to the Speaker of the House and the President of the Senate, by June 30 of each calendar year, a consolidated report, separately listing for each Federal agency the number of records contained in any system of records which were exempted from the application of this section under the provisions of subsections (j) and (k) of this section during the preceding calendar year, and the reasons for the exemptions, and such other information as indicates efforts to administer fully this section.

"(q) EFFECT OF OTHER LAWS.—No agency shall rely on any exemption contained in section 552 of this title to withhold from an individual any record which is otherwise accessible to such individual under the provisions of this section.''

Sec. 4.

The Chapter analysis of chapter 5 of title 5, United States Code, is amended by inserting:

''552a. Records about individuals.''

immediately below:

''552. Public information; agency rules, opinions, orders, and proceedings.''.

Sec. 5.

(a) —
   (1) There is established a Privacy Protection Study Commission (hereinafter referred to as the ''Commission'') which shall be composed of seven members as follows:
      (A) three appointed by the President of the United States,
      (B) two appointed by the President of the Senate, and
      (C) two appointed by the Speaker of the House of Representatives.

   Members of the Commission shall be chosen from among persons who, by reason of their knowledge and expertise in any of the following areas—civil rights and liberties, law, social sciences, computer technology, business, records management, and State and local government—are well qualified for service on the Commission.

   (2) The members of the Commission shall elect a Chairman from among themselves.
   (3) Any vacancy in the membership of the Commission, as long as there are four members in office, shall not impair the power of the Commission but shall be filled in the same manner in which the original appointment was made.

(4) A quorum of the Commission shall consist of a majority of the members, except that the Commission may establish a lower number as a quorum for the purpose of taking testimony. The Commission is authorized to establish such committees and delegate such authority to them as may be necessary to carry out its functions. Each member of the Commission, including the Chairman, shall have equal responsibility and authority in all decisions and actions of the Commission, shall have full access to all information necessary to the performance of their functions, and shall have one vote. Action of the Commission shall be determined by a majority vote of the members present. The Chairman (or a member designated by the Chairman to be acting Chairman) shall be the official spokesman of the Commission in its relations with the Congress, Government agencies, other persons, and the public, and, on behalf of the Commission, shall see to the faithful execution of the administrative policies and decisions of the Commission, and shall report thereon to the Commission from time to time or as the Commission may direct.

(5) —

(A) Whenever the Commission submits any budget estimate or request to the President or the Office of Management and Budget, it shall concurrently transmit a copy of that request to Congress.

(B) Whenever the Commission submits any legislative recommendations, or testimony, or comments on legislation to the President or Office of Management and Budget, it shall concurrently transmit a copy thereof to the Congress. No officer or agency of the United States shall have any authority to require the Commission to submit its legislative recommendations, or testimony, or comments on legislation, to any officer or agency of the United States for approval, comments, or review, prior to the submission of such recommendations, testimony, or comments to the Congress.

(b) The Commission shall—

(1) make a study of the data banks, automated data processing programs, and information systems of governmental, regional, and private organizations, in

order to determine the standards and procedures in force for the protection of personal information; and

(2) recommend to the President and the Congress the extent, if any, to which the requirements and principles of section 552a of title 5, United States Code, should be applied to the information practices of those organizations by legislation, administrative action, or voluntary adoption of such requirements and principles, and report on such other legislative recommendations as it may determine to be necessary to protect the privacy of individuals while meeting the legitimate needs of government and society for information.

(c) —

(1) In the course of conducting the study required under subsection (b)(1) of this section, and in its reports thereon, the Commission may research, examine, and analyze—

(A) interstate transfer of information about individuals that is undertaken through manual files or by computer or other electronic or telecommunications means;

(B) data banks and information programs and systems the operation of which significantly or substantially affect the enjoyment of the privacy and other personal and property rights of individuals;

(C) the use of social security numbers, license plate numbers, universal identifiers, and other symbols to identify individuals in data banks and to gain access to, integrate, or centralize information systems and files; and

(D) the matching and analysis of statistical data, such as Federal census data, with other sources of personal data, such as automobile registries and telephone directories, in order to reconstruct individual responses to statistical questionnaires for commercial or other purposes, in a way which results in a violation of the implied or explicitly recognized confidentiality of such information.

(2) —

(A) The Commission may include in its examination personal information activities in the following areas: medical; insurance; education; employment and personnel; credit, banking and financial institutions; credit bureaus; the commercial reporting industry; cable television and other telecommunications media; travel, hotel and entertainment reservations; and electronic check processing.

(B) The Commission shall include in its examination a study of—

   (i) whether a person engaged in interstate commerce who maintains a mailing list should be required to remove an individual's name and address from such list upon request of that individual;

   (ii) whether the Internal Revenue Service should be prohibited from transfering individually identifiable data to other agencies and to agencies of State governments;

   (iii) whether the Federal Government should be liable for general damages incurred by an individual as the result of a willful or intentional violation of the provisions of sections 552a(g)(1)(C) or (D) of title 5, United States Code; and

   (iv) whether and how the standards for security and confidentiality of records required under section 552a(e)(10) of such title should be applied when a record is disclosed to a person other than an agency.

(C) The Commission may study such other personal information activities necessary to carry out the congressional policy embodied in this Act, except that the commission shall not investigate information systems maintained by religious organizations.

(3) In conducting such study, the Commission shall—

(A) determine what laws, Executive orders, regulations, directives, and judicial decisions govern the activities under study and the extent to which they are consistent with the rights of privacy, due process of law, and other guarantees in the Constitution;

(B) determine to what extent governmental and private information systems affect Federal-State relations or the principle of separation of powers;

(C) examine the standards and criteria governing programs, policies, and practices relating to the collection, soliciting, processing, use, access, integration, dissemination, and transmission of personal information; and

(D) to the maximum extent practicable, collect and utilize findings, reports, studies, hearing transcripts, and recommendations of governmental, legislative and private bodies, institutions, organizations, and individuals which pertain to the problems under study by the Commission.

(d) In addition to its other functions the Commission may—

(1) request assistance of the heads of appropriate departments, agencies, and instrumentalities of the Federal Government, of State and local governments, and other persons in carrying out its functions under this Act;

(2) upon request, assist Federal agencies in complying with the requirements of section 552a of title 5, United States Code;

(3) determine what specific categories of information, the collection of which would violate an individual's right of privacy, should be prohibited by statute from collection by Federal agencies; and

(4) upon request, prepare model legislation for use by State and local governments in establishing procedures for handling, maintaining, and disseminating personal information at the State and local level and provide such technical assistance to State and local governments as they may require in the preparation and implementation of such legislation.

(e) —

(1) The Commission may, in carrying out its functions under this section, conduct such inspections, sit and act at such times and places, hold such hearings, take such testimony, require by subpoena the attendance of such witnesses and the production of such books, records, papers, correspondence, and documents, administer such oaths, have such printing and binding done, and make such expenditures as the Commission deems advisable. A subpoena shall be issued only upon an affirmative vote of a majority of all

members of the Commission. Subpoenas shall be issued under the signature of the Chairman or any member of the Commission designated by the Chairman and shall be served by any person designated by the Chairman or any such member. Any member of the Commission may administer oaths or affirmations to witnesses appearing before the Commission.

(2) —

(A) Each department, agency, and instrumentality of the executive branch of the Government is authorized to furnish to the Commission, upon request made by the Chairman, such information, data, reports and such other assistance as the Commission deems necessary to carry out its functions under this section. Whenever the head of any such department, agency, or instrumentality submits a report pursuant to section 552a(o) of title 5, United States Code, a copy of such report shall be transmitted to the Commission.

(B) In carrying out its functions and exercising its powers under this section, the Commission may accept from any such department, agency, independent instrumentality, or other person any individually identifiable data if such data is necessary to carry out such powers and functions. In any case in which the Commission accepts any such information, it shall assure that the information is used only for the purpose for which it is provided, and upon completion of that purpose such information shall be destroyed or returned to such department, agency, independent instrumentality, or person from which it is obtained, as appropriate.

(3) The Commission shall have the power to—

(A) appoint and fix the compensation of an executive director, and such additional staff personnel as may be necessary, without regard to the provisions of title 5, United States code, governing appointments in the competitive service, and without regard to chapter 51 and subchapter III of chapter 53 of such title relating to classification and General Schedule pay rates, but at rates not in excess of the maximum rate for GS-18 of the General Schedule under section 5332 of such title; and

(B) procure temporary and intermittent services to the same extent as is authorized by section 3109 of title 5, United States Code.

The Commission may delegate any of its functions to such personnel of the Commission as the Commission may designate and may authorize such successive redelegations of such functions as it may deem desirable.

(4) The Commission is authorized—

(A) to adopt, amend, and repeal rules and regulations governing the manner of its operations, organization, and personnel;

(B) to enter into contracts or other arrangements or modifications thereof, with any government, any department, agency, or independent instrumentality of the United States, or with any person, firm, association, or corporation, and such contracts or other arrangements, or modifications thereof, may be entered into without legal consideration, without performance or other bonds, and without regard to section 3709 of the Revised Statutes, as amended (41 U.S.C.5);

(C) to make advance, progress, and other payments which the Commission deems necessary under this Act without regard to the provisions of section 3648 of the Revised Statutes, as amended (31 U.S.C. 529); and

(D) to make such other action as may be necessary to carry out its functions under this section.

(f) —

(1) Each [the] member of the Commission who is an officer or employee of the United States shall serve without additional compensation, but shall continue to receive the salary of his regular position when engaged in the performance of the duties vested in the Commission.

(2) A member of the Commission other than one to whom paragraph (1) applies shall receive per diem at

the maximum daily rate for GS-18 of the General Schedule when engaged in the actual performance of the duties vested in the Commission.

(3) All members of the Commission shall be reimbursed for travel, subsistence, and other necessary expenses incurred by them in the performance of the duties vested in the Commission.

(g) The Commission shall, from time to time, and in an annual report, report to the President and the Congress on its activities in carrying out the provisions of this section. The Commission shall make a final report to the President and to the Congress on its findings pursuant to the study required to be made under subsection (b)(1) of this section not later than two years from the date on which all of the members of the Commission are appointed. The Commission shall cease to exist thirty days after the date on which its final report is submitted to the President and the Congress.

(h) —

(1) Any member, officer, or employee of the Commission, who by virtue of his employment or official position, has possession of, or access to, agency records which contain individually identifiable information the disclosure of which is prohibited by this section, and who knowing that disclosure of the specific material is so prohibited, willfully discloses the material in any manner to any person or agency not entitled to receive it, shall be guilty of a misdemeanor and fined not more than $5,000.

(2) Any person who knowingly and willfully requests or obtains any record concerning an individual from the Commission under false pretenses shall be guilty of a misdemeanor and fined not more than $5,000.

Sec. 6.

The Office of Management and Budget shall—

(1) develop guidelines and regulations for the use of agencies in implementing the provisions of section 552a of title 5, United States Code, as added by section 3 of this Act; and

(2) provide continuing assistance to and oversight of the implementation of the provisions of such section by agencies.

Sec. 7.

(a) —

(1) It shall be unlawful for any Federal, State or local government agency to deny to any individual any right, benefit, or privilege provided by law because of such individual's refusal to disclose his social security account number.

(2) The provisions of paragraph (1) of this subsection shall not apply with respect to—

(A) any disclosure which is required by Federal statute, or

(B) the disclosure of a social security number to any Federal, State, or local agency maintaining a system of records in existence and operating before January 1, 1975, if such disclosure was required under statute or regulation adopted prior to such date to verify the identity of an individual.

(b) Any Federal, State, or local government agency which requests an individual to disclose his social security number to any Federal, State, or local agency maintaining a system of records in existence and operating before January 1, 1975, if such disclosure was required under statute or regulation adopted prior to such date to verify the identity of an individual.

(b) Any Federal, State, or local government agency which requests an individual to disclose his social security account number shall inform that individual whether that disclosure is mandatory or voluntary, by what statutory or other authority such number is solicited, and what uses will be made of it.

Sec. 8.

The provisions of this Act shall be effective on and after the date of enactment, except that the amendments made by section 3 and 4 shall become effective 270 days following the day on which this Act is enacted.

Sec. 9.

There is authorized to be appropriated to carry out the provisions of section 5 of this Act for fiscal years 1975, 1976, and 1977 the sum of $1,500,000, except that not more than $750,000 may be expended during any such fiscal year.

Approved December 31, 1974

LEGISLATIVE HISTORY:

HOUSE REPORT No. 93–1416 accompanying H. R. 16373 (Comm. on Government Operations).
SENATE REPORT No. 93–1183 (Comm. on Government Operations).
CONGRESSIONAL RECORD, Vol. 120 (1974):

- Nov. 21, considered and passed Senate.
- Dec. 11, considered and passed House, amended, in lieu of H.R. 16373
- Dec. 17, Senate concurred in House amendment with amendments.
- Dec. 18, House concurred in Senate amendments.

WEEKLY COMPILATION OF PRESIDENTIAL DOCUMENTS, Vol. 11, NO. 1: Jan. 1, Presidential statement.

Appendix D

RESOLUTIONS COMPLEMENTARY TO THE MASS MEDIA DECLARATION ADOPTED BY THE TWENTIETH GENERAL CONFERENCE OF UNESCO—NOVEMBER 1978*

AMENDMENT TO THE UNESCO DRAFT PROGRAMME AND BUDGET FOR 1979-1980 (DOCUMENT 20 C/5)
(Adopted by acclamation 22 November 1978)

Resolution submitted by: Australia, France, Sri Lanka, Tunisia, USA and Venezuela.

The General Conference,

Conscious of the need to mobilize and to secure maximum value from all possible co-operation and assistance for the development of communications and information systems in order to promote a free flow and a wider and better balanced exchange of information,

Noting with appreciation the increasing willingness on the

---

* The resolutions were distributed at the Online Conferences, Ltd. Data Regulation Conference in November 1978 by Roland S. Hornet, Jr., Director of International Communications Policy, International Communications Agency, U.S.A.

part of governments and institutions to co-operate in this process and to provide practical assistance,

Recalling the medium-term plan and guidance notes concerning the development of communications,

Emphasizing the constructive potential of UNESCO for international co-operation in respect of communications and information,

Requests the Director-General to intensify the encouragement of communications development and to hold consultations designed to lead to the provision to developing countries of technological and other means for promoting a free flow and a wider and better balanced exchange of information of all kinds;

Invites the Director-General for this purpose, to convene as early as possible after the conclusion of this twentieth session of the General Conference a planning meeting of representatives of governments, to develop a proposal for institutional arrangements to systematize collaborative consultation on communications development activities, needs and plans;

Authorizes him, in light of the recommendations of this planning meeting, to take the necessary steps to foster such institutional arrangements and for this purpose to seek the partnership of other appropriate international bodies.

INTERIM REPORT OF THE INTERNATIONAL COMMISSION FOR THE STUDY OF COMMUNICATION PROBLEMS (DOCUMENT 20 C/94) (Adopted by acclamation 22 November 1978)

Resolution submitted by: France, Sri Lanka, Tunisia, USA and Venezuela.

The General Conference,

Emphasizing the significance of the work of the International Commission for the study of communication problems and appreciating the efforts so far made, as given concrete expression in the interim report.

Recalling Resolution 4.142 adopted by the General Conference in Nairobi requesting the Director-General to encourage co-operative measures that would strengthen the information and communication systems of developing countries in accordance with their needs,

Conscious of the aspirations of the developing countries for the establishment of a new, more just and more effective world information and communication order,

Taking into consideration the widely shared hope that UNESCO contribute effectively to the creation of a world order of information tending to establish balanced relations and exchanges among all countries,

Reaffirming the evident necessity to change the situation of dependence of the developing world in the field of information and communication, and to replace it with relationships of interdependence and cooperation,

Noting the benefits that might accrue to the peoples of the developed countries, and of the world, from an expanded opportunity to hear the authentic voice of differing societies and cultures in a dialogue made progressively more equal,

Taking into account the activities of the various organisms serving the developing countries in their quest for strengthening the information and communications systems in their own countries,

Conscious also of the contributions made by certain institutions of the developed countries, and of the importance of the further contributions that they can make, to the realization of this objective,

Invites the Director-General to request the members of the International Commission for the Study of Communication Problems to address themselves, in the course of preparing their final report, to the analysis and proposal of concrete and practical measures leading to the establishment of a more just and effective world information order,

Invites all member countries of UNESCO, and all non-governmental organizations affiliated with UNESCO or contributing to its work, to extend their advice and co-operation to this work of the commission, without interference to preparations and actions concurrently being undertaken in this field by the United Nations or its international Specialized Agencies,

Requests the Director-General to organize at the Twenty-First Session of the UNESCO General Conference, procedures for consideration of the final report of the Commission that will permit representatives of the United Nations, its international Specialized Agencies, and relevant non-governmental organizations, to contribute their perspectives towards the formulation of the appropriate actions to be taken in order to move towards the realization of a more just and effective world information order.

Appendix E

GUIDELINES SUBMITTED TO THE OECD BY THE UNITED STATES AND AN APPARENT RESPONSE BY THE OECD SECRETARIAT*

I *Statement of Objectives*

In the context of the OECD Declaration on International Investment and Multinational Enterprises of 1976 and other relevant Agreements of OECD, to establish international Guidelines for national administration of personal data protection, to promote the free flow of information, the protection of personal liberties and free trade.

II *Principles of Personal Data Protection*

Without prejudice to further developments in international law and international cooperation in relation to transfrontier flows of personal data, member countries, so far as compatible with domestic law and policy, should be guided in their national privacy protection policy by the principles concerning protection of personal privacy contained herein.

1. There shall be no personal-data record-keeping

---

* These guidelines were distributed to the TDF interest group by Herbert E. Marks of the Washington law firm of Wilkinson, Cragun and Barker.

system whose very existence is secret and there shall be a policy of openness about an organization's personal data record-keeping policies, practices, and systems.

2. An individual about whom information is maintained by a record-keeping organization in individually identifiable form shall have a right to see and copy that information. (The Individual Access Principle)

3. An individual about whom information is maintained by a record-keeping organization shall have a right to correct or amend the substance of that information. (The Individual Participation Principle)

4. There shall be limits on the types of information an organization may collect about an individual, as well as certain requirements with respect to the manner in which it collects such information (The Collection Limitation Principle)

5. There shall be limits on the internal uses of information about an individual within a record-keeping organization. (The Use Limitation Principle)

6. There shall be limits on the external disclosures of information about an individual a record-keeping organization may make. (The Disclosure Limitation Principle)

7. A record-keeping organization shall bear an affirmative responsibility for establishing reasonable and proper information management policies and practices which assure that its collection, maintenance, use, and dissemination of information about an individual is necessary and lawful and that the information itself is current and accurate. (The Information Management Principle)

8. A record-keeping organization shal. be accountable for its personal-data record-keeping policies, practices and systems. (The Accountability Principle)

III *Guidelines Relating to Transborder Flows of Personal Data*
So far as feasible:

1. governments should undertake to promote these principles both domestically and internationally;

2. governments should provide procedures or institutions to focus on, review and make recommendations with respect to domestic implementation of these guidelines;

3. governments should consider the establishment of procedures or institutions to enforce personal privacy protection law or policy;

4. governments should support and encourage the development of codes of conduct adopting the 8 principles listed above by private sector firms or associations;

5. governments should undertake to ensure, to the greatest extent possible, the uninterrupted free flow of information;

6. governments should undertake to avoid the unjustified disruption of international trade patterns and the creation of non-tariff barriers that would interfere with transborder data flows;

7. governments should refrain from restricting the import and export of data unless doing so is essential to the protection of vital national security interests; and

8. government involvement should be no more extensive than is reasonably required for the protection of personal data and is consistent with the objective of promoting the free transborder flow of data.

IV *Guidelines Relating to Cooperation Among Countries on Issues of Jurisdiction and Reciprocity*
1. If deemed appropriate, governments should work toward the establishment of international law to govern conflict of law issues.

2. Governments should consider adopting the principle that, in a choice of law situation, that law offering the greatest personal privacy protection shall govern.

3. Governments should consider the desirability of according foreign data or data on foreign nationals no less protection than that accorded domestic data.

V *International Cooperation*
1. Differing national privacy protection policies are the result of many factors, such as differing legal sys-

tems, social priorities and public policies. In view of these differences, harmonization is desirable, though it may be difficult to achieve in practice.

2. Governments should continue to pursue harmonization of national privacy protection laws, taking into account practical experience with existing guidelines, technological innovation and the desirability of increasing cooperation, and with particular emphasis on the development of uniform procedural mechanisms and compatible compliance requirements.

3. Consultations on the above-mentioned principles should be pursued. In connection with the application of these guiding principles, a specific mechanism of consultation and/or notification or some other appropriate form of action should be determined as soon as possible, taking into account the work done by other international organizations.

EXPERT GROUP ON TRANSBORDER DATA BARRIERS AND THE PROTECTION OF PRIVACY

First Draft Guidelines on Basic Rules Governing the Transborder Flow and the Protection of Personal Data and Privacy

1. At its 1st meeting the Expert Group agreed that a Drafting Group should be set up to develop the guidelines indicated in Point 4(i) of the Group's Mandate (DSTI/ICCP/ 78.6).

2. A Summary Record of the first meting of the Drafting Group, held in Stockholm on 10th-12th July, 1978, has been circulated under reference number DSTI/ICCP/78.22[DG-6].

3. The attached First Draft of the Guidelines is based on the deliberations of the Drafting Group. It is submitted to the Expert Group for comments and discussions of *substance.* Proposed modifications in *detail,* on the other hand, should be sent to the Secretariat *in writing* not later than 30th November next, for submission to the Drafting Group which

will hold its second meeting on 7th and 8th December, 1978, i.e. immediately following that of the Expert Group.

First Draft Guidelines On Basic Rules Governing The Transborder Flow And The Protection Of Personal Data And Privacy

THE COUNCIL

Having regard to Articles 1(c), 3(a), and 5(b) of the Convention of the Organisation for Economic Co-operation and Development of 14th December, 1960;

Recognising:

> that automatic processing and transborder movements of personal data create new forms of interdependence among countries and accompanying needs to reconcile fundamental but competing values and develop compatible rules and practices;
>
> that transborder movements of personal data are essential to economic, scientific, educational, and social development;
>
> that Member countries have a common interest in protecting privacy and individual liberties with regard to automatic processing of personal data, in particular the right of privacy of individuals;

Determined to promote the free flow of information and to avoid the creation of unjustified obstacles to the development of world trade and scientific and cultural relations among countries:

RECOMMENDS

I. That Member countries take into account in their domestic legislation the principles concerning automated processing of personal data set forth in the Annex to this Recommendation which is an integral part of it;

II. That Member countries should develop their cooperation in regard to automated processing of personal data as outlined in the Guidelines set forth in the Annex.

ANNEX

First Draft Guidelines On Basic Rules Governing The Transborder Flow And The Protection Of Personal Data And Privacy

I. INTRODUCTION

1. For the purposes of these Guidelines:

   (a) "automatic processing" means the processing of data largely performed by computers as defined in the ISO data processing vocabulary Section 01 (ISO 2382/I-1974);

   (b) "Country" means any Member country which participates in this Recommendation;

   (c) "data controller" means any record-keeper responsible for the management of systems for the automatic processing of personal data;

   (d) "data management" includes the collection, maintenance, use, and dissemination of data;

   (e) "innocent transit of data" means movement of personal data across the territory of a Country without involving their use, or storage with a view to use, in that Country;

   (f) "personal data" means any item or grouping of information related to identified or identifiable individuals ("data subjects");

   (g) "record" means a unit of personal data;

   (h) "system" means an organised collection of people, machines, and data processing procedures;

   (i) "transborder movement of data" refers to movements of data across national borders in machine-readable form.

2. Subject to the limitations set out in Section II, Title C, paragraph 16, these Guidelines apply to automatic processing of personal data in the public and private sector.

3. Countries may, possibly on the basis of reciprocity, apply these Guidelines to personal data which are processed by other than automatic means.

4. These Guidelines are to be interpreted, and where ap-

propriate implemented, with due regard for national interests of sovereignty, security, and public policy ("ordre public").

5. These Guidelines are not intended to prejudice other applicable international agreements and do not preclude any more favourable measures for the protection of personal data. They are to be supplemented and further developed within the framework of activities undertaken by the OECD and by other appropriate international organisations.

II. GUIDELINES RELATING TO BASIC RULES ON THE ESTABLISHMENT AND OPERATION OF SYSTEMS FOR THE AUTOMATIC PROCESSING OF PERSONAL DATA

Title A—Fair Record-Keeping Principles
6. There should be no systems for the automatic processing of personal data whose very existence is secret and there should be a policy of openness about developments, practices and policies in such systems.

7. Personal data should be obtained and recorded by fair and lawful means and there should be limits to the types of information an organisation may collect about an individual.

8. Personal data should be stored for specific purposes and there should be corresponding limits to the use of such data by the record-keeping organisation.

9. Personal data should be relevant to the purpose of the data processing system, as well as accurate and, where necessary, kept up-to-date.

10. There should be limits to the external disclosures of information that a record-keeping organisation may make about an individual.

11. Systems for the automatic processing of personal data should be protected by reasonable security safeguards against accidental or malicious loss, modification or disclosure of data.

12. Personal data should not be stored in individually identifiable form or in machine-readable form longer than is required for the attainment of the purpose of the record.

13. A record-keeper responsible for the management of a system for the automatic processing of personal data should, as data controller, be accountable for its record-keeping policies, practices and systems and bear an affirmative responsibility for establishing policies and practices which reflect the principles stated in Title A.

Title B—Basic Rights of Data Subjects

14. Individuals should have a right to obtain information about the existence, the purpose and, to a reasonable extent, the use of systems for the automatic processing of personal data.

15. Data subjects or, where appropriate, their representatives should have a right:

(a) to obtain information about the existence of a record on them;

(b) to gain access to and review, in easily intelligible form, records pertaining to them;

(c) to challenge records pertaining to them that in their opinion are not lawful, accurate, relevant or complete.

Title C—Implementation

16. So far as consistent with domestic law and policy, and with as few as possible, clearly stated exceptions, Countries undertake to promote the principles set out in Titles A and B above. In implementing these principles domestically, Countries should in particular:

(a) consider the establishment of procedures or institutions for the protection of privacy and individual liberties in respect of systems for the automatic processing of personal data;

(b) provide for

(i) readily available opportunities for data subjects of their representatives to initiate proceedings aimed at preventing use of systems for the automatic processing of personal data which violate their rights,

(ii) adequate remedies in case of such violations;

(c) encourage and support self-regulation, for example in the form of codes of professional conduct for persons and organisations involved in automatic processing of personal data;

(d) avoid discrimination between data subjects on the basis of nationality, domicile or residence.

17. The principles stated in Titles A and B are to be regarded as minimum rules and Countries should consider the needs and advantages of developing and implementing more far-reaching measures

III. GUIDELINES RELATING TO THE TRANS-BORDER MOVEMENT OF PERSONAL DATA

18. Countries should:

(a) take all necessary steps to ensure continuous and secure transborder movement of personal data and the observance of freedom of innocent transit of such data;

(b) refrain from preventing or restricting transborder movements of personal data between Countries unless such movements:

  (i) are contrary to laws on domestic processing of personal data,

  (ii) would considerably weaken the protection of data required by the Country where the data originated;

(c) refrain from developing policies and practices exceeding those required for the reasonable protection of personal data and inconsistent with the objective of promoting free transborder data movements.

IV. GUIDELINES RELATING TO CO-OPERATION AMONG COUNTRIES, JURISDICTIONAL PROBLEMS, AND CONFLICTS OF LAWS

19. Countries undertake to exchange information on matters related to these Guidelines and, in particular, to consider the establishment of national representatives or procedures to facilitate such information exchange as well as mutual aid and support in procedural and investigative matters.

20. Countries should work towards a progressive harmonisa-

tion of national laws and practices relating to the protection of privacy and individual liberties in systems for the automatic processing of personal data. In doing so, care should be taken to make known and accessible the detailed implementation of provisions of a general nature and to ensure that procedural mechanisms and compliance requirements regarding transborder movements of personal data are simple and compatible.

21. Countries should take into consideration the implications for other Countries of the establishment and use of systems for the automatic processing of personal data, particularly where the establishment of such systems in one Country would result in a circumvention of the domestic legislation of other Countries or would affect a large number of their nationals.

22. With regard to conflicts of laws involving transborder movements of personal data, Countries should consider adopting the following principles:

(a) At the option of the data subject, and to the extent that effective judgements and other legal decisions are possible, proceedings aimed at preventing or remedying violation of the principles and rights set out in Section II of these Guidelines may be initiated in:

   (i) the Country or Countries where data are ordinarily stored;

  (ii) the Country where or from which main control over data is exercised;

 (iii) the Country in which the data controller has his main residence or principal place of business;

 (iv) the Country where a wrong was committed or completed.

(b) The choice of substantive law in matters related to Titles A and B in Section III of these Guidelines should as far as possible give preference to the law offering the greatest protection of personal data.

23. For the application of these Guidelines, a specific mechanism of consultation and co-operation should be determined as soon as possible, taking into account the work done by other international organisations.

Appendix F

REVISED PRELIMINARY DRAFT OF THE INTERNATIONAL CONVENTION VIS-A-VIS AUTOMATED RECORDS*

COUNCIL OF EUROPE
COMMITTEE OF EXPERTS ON DATA PROTECTION

Working Group A—International Convention

Revised preliminary draft
INTERNATIONAL CONVENTION ON THE PROTECTION OF INDIVIDUALS VIS-A-VIS AUTOMATED RECORDS

(drawn up by the Secretariat in the light of conclusions of the 2nd meeting of the Committee of experts on data protection, 26–29 Sept. 1977)

Strasbourg, 6 January 1978

Preamble

The States signatory to this Convention,

Having regard to the growing movement across frontiers of automatically processed personal information,

Considering that it is desirable to ensure for every person the protection of his fundamental rights, liberties and essential interests vis-a-vis such data flows,

Concerned at the same time not to restrict the free interna-

---

* This report was distributed to the TDF interest group by Herbert E. Marks of the Washington law firm of Wilkinson, Cragun and Barker.

tional flow of information, nor to place barriers in the way of economic development or international commerce,
Have agreed as follows:

CHAPTER I—GENERAL PROVISIONS

Article 1

For the purpose of this Convention:

(a) "personal data" shall mean: any information relating to identified or identifiable natural persons ("data subjects");

(b) "automated record" shall mean: any set or system of information which is processed automatically;

(c) "automatic processing" shall include the following operations: storage of data, carrying out of logical and arithmetic operations on those data, alteration, erasure and dissemination of data;

(d) shall be regarded as "controller of the record": the person, body or agency who is empowered to decide what processing operations are performed on personal data;

(e) shall be regarded as "manager of the record": the person, body or agency who is instructed by the controller of the record to carry out the processing operations on personal data.

Article 2

1. This Convention shall apply to personal data which are the subject of automatic processing in the public and private sector.

2. Each Contracting State may, at the time of signature or when depositing its instrument of ratification, acceptance, approval or accession, or at any later time, indicate, by a declaration addressed to the depositary of this Convention, that it will extend the provisions concerning natural persons to groups, associations, foundations, companies or other organizations of natural persons, whether or not these are legal persons. This State may specify in the declaration that it is conditional on reciprocity.

This declaration shall take effect with regard to other Contracting States three months after its reception by the Secretary General of the Council of Europe.

It may be withdrawn or modified on the same conditions.

CHAPTER II—MINIMUM RULES OF DATA PROTECTION

Article 3

1. The Contracting States undertake to enforce in their territory observance of the minimum rules set out in paragraph 2 of this Article, so as to ensure that when personal data are processed automatically, the rights, liberties and essential interests of data subjects, whatever their nationality, residence or domicile, shall be duly respected.

2. Particular provisions must be adopted in order to ensure:
   (a) that every person can discover the existence of an automated personal record and the identity of the controller of the record;
   (b) that every person is enabled to obtain from the controller of the record, or any other person specifically appointed for the purpose:
      i) knowledge of the existence or non-existence of personal data relating to him contained in the automated record;
      ii) communication of such data, if any;
      iii) any correction or erasure, where necessary, of data recorded in violation of the provisions of subparagraphs (c) and (d) below;
   (c) that personal data are collected lawfully and fairly, are accurate and, where necessary, kept up-to-date, as well as appropriate and relevant to the purpose of the record;
   (d) that data which reflect racial origin, philosophical, religious, political or trade union views shall not be recorded save with the data subject's consent or unless expressly authorized by virtue of a law or regulation issued in conformity with the legal system of each Contracting State;
   (e) that apart from the general measures of security applicable to all computer installations, special measures should be taken to protect personal data stored in an automated record against accidental or willful loss or destruction as well as against unauthorized access, alteration or release.

3. The Contracting States shall admit no exceptions to the provisions set out in paragraph 2 above, other than by virtue of the legal rules on secrecy or confidentiality.

Article 4

The Contracting States shall observe the following rules with regard to automatic processing of personal data affecting data subjects residing abroad or involving data processing operations in the territory of one or several other States.

1. The security rules set out in Article 3, paragraph 2(e) shall be enforced by each Contracting State in whose territory hardware, software or data belonging to an automated personal record are located;

2. Where a data subject resides in a Contracting State other than that in which personal data relating to him are being processed automatically, it shall be permitted that steps to ensure compliance with the provisions of Article 3 are taken either directly in the Contracting State in which the controller of the automated record, or where appropriate, the manager of this record, resides or indirectly, through the intermediary of authority designated in conformity with Article 5, by the Contracting State where the data subject resides.

3. Where the processing of an automated personal record involves operations in the territory of several Contracting States, the latter shall take all necessary steps in order that one single controller of the record is appointed who is to be domiciled in the Contracting State which is his principal place of business or his habitual residence (State of domicile).

In that case, the authority designated by the State of domicile in conformity with Article 5 may ask the cooperation of the authorities designated by the other Contracting States in order to ensure compliance with the provisions set out in Article 3.

CHAPTER III—COOPERATION BETWEEN CONTRACTING STATES

Article 5

1. The Contracting States undertake to render each other mutual assistance in order to facilitate the implementation of this Convention.

To that end, each Contracting State shall designate one or several authorities whose name and address it shall communicate to the depositary of this Convention.

2. The authority designated by a Contracting State shall in particular carry out the following functions on the request of an authority designated by another Contracting State:

(a) furnish information on the law and regulations of the requested State as well as factual information with regard to the keeping and processing of automated personal records in its territory;

(b) verify the presumed existence in the territory of the requested State of an automated personal record or a part thereof, or an installation or device processing such a record;

(c) make observations, and investigations, as specified in the request, with regard to such a record, installation or device;

(d) transmit to the controller or manager of an automated personal record any application made by a person in another Contracting State in accordance with the provisions of Article 3, paragraph 2 (b).

3. The request for assistance shall contain all of the necessary information on the substance and the purpose of the matter. It shall in any case mention where it is made on the requesting authority's own behalf or on behalf of a data subject residing in the Contracting State from which the request emanates.

4. The authority designated by one Contracting State which has received information from the authority designated by another Contracting State, either in support of a request for assistance or in reply to a request for assistance it has formulated itself, shall not use that information for purposes other than those specified in the request for assistance.

Moreover, the persons belonging to or employed by an authority designated by a Contracting State shall be bound by the same restrictions of secrecy or confidentiality with regard to that information as the persons belonging to or employed by the corresponding authority in another Contracting State.

5. The designated authority may refuse a request for assistance if:

(a) this is not compatible with its own power or with any other provisions of data protection law of the requested State;

(b) it considers that:

i) the request does not conform to the provisions of this Convention, or

ii) compliance would interfere with the sovereignty, security, public policy or other vital interest of the requested State, or with rights, liberties, or essential interest of persons under its jurisdiction.

6. The provisions of this Convention shall not restrict the freedom of Contracting States to render each other mutual assistance through diplomatic or consular channels.

Article 6

1. Subject to the provisions of paragraph 2 below, assistance given by an authority designated by one Contracting State to an authority designated by another Contracting State shall not give rise to any refund of fees or costs in connection with the services rendered.

2. The sums due to experts and interpreters specially employed to assist an authority designated by one Contracting State in the fulfillment of a request for assistance from the authority designated by another Contracting State shall be borne by the requesting authority.

3. The data subject may be charged no other fees or costs in connection with the steps taken on his behalf in another Contracting State with a view to the application of the provisions laid down in Article 3 than those lawfully payable by residents of that State.

Article 7

1. A Standing Consultative Committee shall be set up within a year of the entry into force of this Convention. This Committee may formulate proposals to the governments of the Contracting States, designed to improve the practical im-

plementation of the Convention and, if necessary, to amend or supplement its provisions.

2. In the event of differences of opinion arising over the interpretation or application of the provisions of Articles 3 and 4 of this Convention, the Committee shall endeavor to settle such differences between the Contracting States at the request of any one of them.

3. Each Contracting State shall appoint a representative to this Committee (Each State which has signed but not yet ratified the Convention may be represented by an observer).

4. The Committee shall be convened by the depositary of this Convention. Its first session shall take place within six months of the date of its establishment. Subsequent sessions shall be held at least every three years.

5. The Standing Consultative Committee shall draw up its own rules of procedure.

CHAPTER IV—RECOGNITION AND ENFORCEMENT OF DECISIONS— PROVISIONS OF DOMESTIC LAW AND INTERNATIONAL LAW

Article 8

1. Any decision, ruling, injunction or judgment made in any Contracting State for the protection of a data subject in relation to a controller or manager of an automated personal record shall be recognized or declared enforceable in another Contracting State if it is no longer subject to ordinary forms of review in the State of origin.

Provisionally enforceable decisions and provisional measures shall, although subject to ordinary forms of review, be recognized or enforced in another Contracting State if similar decisions may be rendered and enforced in that State.

2. Recognition or enforcement of a decision may, however, be refused:

    (a) if recognition or enforcement of the decision is manifestly incompatible with the public policy ('ordre public') of the requested State addressed; or

(b) if proceedings between the same parties and having the same purpose are pending before an authority of another Contracting State;

(c) if the decision is incompatible with a decision rendered between the same parties and having the same purpose, in another State.

3. Without prejudice to the provisions of paragraph 2, a decision rendered by default shall be recognized or enforced only if notice of the institution of the proceedings, including notice of the substance of the claim, has been served on the defaulting party in accordance with the law of the State of origin and if, having regard to the circumstances, that party has had sufficient time to enable him to defend the proceedings.

Article 9

Nothing in this Convention shall prevent a Contracting State from giving a wider measure of protection to the data subjects than is provided for in this Convention.

Article 10

Nothing in this Convention shall affect existing or future international agreements and other practices and arrangements between Contracting States which relate to matters dealt with in this Convention.

CHAPTER V—FINAL CLAUSES
(to be detailed)

Article 11

Opening to signature/ratification/depositary of the Convention and of instruments/entry into force.

Article 12

Accessions and their entry into force.

Article 13

Territorial clause.

Article 14

Reservations.

Article 15

Denunciation.

Article 16

Notifications by the depositary to Contracting States concerning: signatures, ratifications, entry into force, territorial clauses, reservations, denunciation and notifications received in pursuance of Articles 2(2) and 5(1).

Appendix G
THE EUROPEAN CONVENTION ON HUMAN RIGHTS*

FOREWORD

Drawn up within the Council of Europe, the European Convention on Human Rights was signed on 4 November 1950 and came into force on 3 September 1953[1].

All 20 of the member States of the Council of Europe have signed it, and, with the exception of Portugal and Spain, also ratified it[2].

The European Convention on Human Rights represents a collective guarantee at a European level of a number of principles set out in the Universal Declaration of Human Rights, supported by international judicial machinery making decisions which must be respected by contracting States.

This international guarantee is not a substitute for national guarantees of fundamental rights, but is supplementary to them. Proceedings before the organs created by the Convention cannot be instituted until after all domestic remedies have been exhausted.

These organs are the European Commission and Court of

[1] Five protocols have since been adopted, of which Nos. 3 and 5 modify the text of the Convention itself. Since these modifications have been incorporated into the text of the Convention, these Protocols, unlike 1, 2 and 4, are not included in the Appendix.
[2] See chart showing Ratifications and Optional Declarations, p. 192.
* Reprinted with blanket protection of the Council of Europe.

Human Rights, which have their seat in Strasbourg. Furthermore, the Committee of Ministers of the Council of Europe may be called upon to act in cases which are not brought before the European Court.

The Commission may receive petitions from a Contracting Party alleging violations of rights and freedoms set forth in the Convention by another Contracting State. Moreover any person, group of individuals or non-governmental Organisation may also address petitions to the Commission against the Contracting Party within whose jurisdiction he or they fall, as long as that Contracting Party has recognised, by express declaration, the competence of the Commission to receive such petitions[2].

The Commission has mainly a mission of inquiry and conciliation. If no friendly settlement has been reached on the basis of respect for Human Rights, the Commission formulates a legal opinion and, as regards the subsequent procedure, the Commission has the right, along with the States concerned, of referring the case to the Court.

The Court, for its part, is competent to take a judicial decision, which is binding on the parties to the action, on whether in a given case the Convention has or has not been violated by a Contracting State.

If the Court is not seized of the case, it is for the Committee of Ministers to decide on the question.

Any additional information may be obtained from the following address:

Directorate of Human Rights
Council of Europe
F-67006 Strasbourg Cedex

CONVENTION FOR THE PROTECTION
OF HUMAN RIGHTS
AND FUNDAMENTAL FREEDOMS

The Governments signatory hereto, being Members of the Council of Europe,

Considering the Universal Declaration of Human Rights proclaimed by the General Assembly of the United Nations on 10th December 1948;

Considering that this Declaration aims at securing the universal and effective recognition and observance of the Rights therein declared;

Considering that the aim of the Council of Europe is the achievement of greater unity between its Members and that one of the methods by which that aim is to be pursued is the maintenance and further realisation of Human Rights and Fundamental Freedoms;

Reaffirming their profound belief in those Fundamental Freedoms which are the foundation of justice and peace in the world and are best maintained on the one hand by an effective political democracy and on the other by a common understanding and observance of the Human Rights upon which they depend;

Being resolved, as the Governments of European countries which are likeminded and have a common heritage of political traditions, ideals, freedom and the rule of law to take the first steps for the collective enforcement of certain of the Rights stated in the Universal Declaration,

Have agreed as follows:

Article 1

The High Contracting Parties shall secure to everyone within their jurisdiction the rights and freedoms defined in Section 1 of this Convention.

SECTION I

Article 2

1. Everyone's right to life shall be protected by law. No one shall be deprived of his life intentionally save in the execution of a sentence of a court following his conviction of a crime for which this penalty is provided by law.

2. Deprivation of life shall not be regarded as inflicted in contravention of this Article when it results from the use of force which is no more than absolutely necessary:

(a) in defence of any person from unlawful violence;

(b) in order to effect a lawful arrest or to prevent the escape of a person lawfully detained;

(c) in action lawfully taken for the purpose of quelling a riot or insurrection.

Article 3

No one shall be subjected to torture or to inhuman or degrading treatment or punishment.

Article 4

1. No one shall be held in slavery or servitude.

2. No one shall be required to perform forced or compulsory labour.

3. For the purpose of this Article the term "forced or compulsory labour" shall not include:

(a) any work required to be done in the ordinary course of detention imposed according to the provisions of Article 5 of this Convention or during conditional release from such detention;

(b) any service of a military character or, in case of conscientious objectors in countries where they are recognised, service exacted instead of compulsory military service;

(c) any service exacted in case of an emergency or calamity threatening the life or well-being of the community;

(d) any work or service which forms part of normal civic obligations.

Article 5

1. Everyone has the right to liberty and security of person.

No one shall be deprived of his liberty save in the following cases and in accordance with a procedure prescribed by law;

(a) the lawful detention of a person after conviction by a competent court;

(b) the lawful arrest or detention of a person for non-compliance with the lawful order of a court or in order to secure the fulfilment of any obligation prescribed by law;

(c) the lawful arrest or detention of a person effected for the purpose of bringing him before the competent legal authority on reasonable suspicion of having committed an offence or when it is reasonably considered necessary to prevent his committing an offence or fleeing after having done so;

(d) the detention of a minor by lawful order for the purpose of educational supervision or his lawful detention for the purpose of bringing him before the competent legal authority;

(e) the lawful detention of persons for the prevention of the spreading of infectious diseases, of persons of unsound mind, alcoholics or drug addicts or vagrants;

(f) the lawful arrest or detention of a person to prevent his effecting an unauthorised entry into the country or of a person against whom action is being taken with a view to deportation or extradition.

2. Everyone who is arrested shall be informed promptly, in a language which he understands, of the reasons for his arrest and of any charge against him.

3. Everyone arrested or detained in accordance with the provisions of paragraph 1 *(c)* of this Article shall be brought promptly before a judge or other officer authorised by law to exercise judicial power and shall be entitled to trial within a reasonable time or to release pending trial. Release may be conditioned by guarantees to appear for trial.

4. Everyone who is deprived of his liberty by arrest or detention shall be entitled to take proceedings by which the

lawfulness of his detention shall be decided speedily by a court and his release ordered if the detention is not lawful.

5. Everyone who has been the victim of arrest or detention in contravention of the provisions of this Article shall have an enforceable right to compensation.

Article 6

1. In the determination of his civil rights and obligations or of any criminal charge against him, everyone is entitled to a fair and public hearing within a reasonable time by an independent and impartial tribunal established by law. Judgment shall be pronounced publicly but the press and public may be excluded from all or part of the trial in the interest of morals, public order or national security in a democratic society, where the interests of juveniles or the protection of the private life of the parties so require, or to the extent strictly necessary in the opinion of the court in special circumstances where publicity would prejudice the interests of justice.

2. Everyone charged with a criminal offence shall be presumed innocent until proved guilty according to law.

3. Everyone charged with a criminal offence has the following minimum rights;

(a) to be informed promptly, in a language which he understands and in detail, of the nature and cause of the accusation against him:

(b) to have adequate time and facilities for the preparation of his defence;

(c) to defend himself in person or through legal assistance of his own choosing or, if he has not sufficient means to pay for legal assistance, to be given it free when the interests of justice so require;

(d) to examine or have examined witnesses against him and to obtain the attendance and examination of witnesses on his behalf under the same conditions as witnesses against him;

(e) to have the free assistance of an interpreter if he cannot understand or speak the language used in court.

Article 7

1. No one shall be held guilty of any criminal offence on account of any act or omission which did not constitute a criminal offence under national or international law at the time when it was committed. Nor shall a heavier penalty be imposed than the one that was applicable at the time the criminal offence was committed.

2. This Article shall not prejudice the trial and punishment of any person for any act or omission which at the time when it was committed, was criminal according to the general principles of law recognised by civilised nations.

Article 8

1. Everyone has the right to respect for his private and family life, his home and his correspondence.

2. There shall be no interference by a public authority with the exercise of this right except such as is in accordance with the law and is necessary in a democratic society in the interests of national security, public safety or the economic well-being of the country, for the prevention of disorder or crime, for the protection of health or morals, or for the protection of the rights and freedoms of others.

Article 9

1. Everyone has the right to freedom of thought, conscience and religion; this right includes freedom to change his religion or belief and freedom, either alone or in community with others and in public or private, to manifest his religion or belief, in worship, teaching, practice and observance.

2. Freedom to manifest one's religion or beliefs shall be subject only to such limitations as are prescribed by law and are necessary in a democratic society in the interests of public safety, for the protection of public order, health or morals, or for the protection of the rights and freedoms of others.

Article 10

1. Everyone has the right to freedom of expression. This right shall include freedom to hold opinions and to receive

and impart information and ideas without interference by public authority and regardless of frontiers. This Article shall not prevent States from requiring the licensing of broadcasting, television or cinema enterprises.

2. The exercise of these freedoms, since it carries with it duties and responsibilities, may be subject to such formalities, conditions, restrictions or penalties as are prescribed by law and are necessary in a democratic society, in the interests of national security, territorial integrity or public safety, for the prevention of disorder or crime, for the protection of health or morals, for the protection of the reputation or rights of others, for preventing the disclosure of information received in confidence, or for maintaining the authority and impartiality of the judiciary.

Article 11

1. Everyone has the right to freedom of peaceful assembly and to freedom of association with others, including the right to form and to join trade unions for the protection of his interests.

2. No restrictions shall be placed on the exercise of these rights other than such as are prescribed by law and are necessary in a democratic society in the interests of national security or public safety, for the prevention of disorder or crime, for the protection of health or morals or for the protection of the rights and freedoms of others. This Article shall not prevent the imposition of lawful restrictions on the exercise of these rights by members of the armed forces, of the police or of the administration of the State.

Article 12

Men and women of marriageable age have the right to marry and to found a family, according to the national laws governing the exercise of this right.

Article 13

Everyone whose rights and freedoms as set forth in this Convention are violated shall have an effective remedy before a national authority not withstanding that the violation has been committed by persons acting in an official capacity.

Article 14

The enjoyment of the rights and freedoms set forth in this Convention shall be secured without discrimination on any ground such as sex, race, colour, language, religion, political or other opinion, national or social origin, association with a national minority, property, birth or other status.

Article 15

1. In time of war or other public emergency threatening the life of the nation any High Contracting Party may take measures derogating from its obligations under this Convention to the extent strictly required by the exigencies of the situation provided that such measures are not inconsistent with its other obligations under international law.

2. No derogation from Article 2, except in respect of deaths resulting from lawful acts of war, or from Articles 3, 4 (paragraph 1) and 7 shall be made under this provision.

3. Any High Contracting Party availing itself of this right of derogation shall keep the Secretary General of the Council of Europe fully informed of the measures which it has taken and the reasons therefor. It shall also inform the Secretary General of the Council of Europe when such measures have ceased to operate and the provisions of the Convention are again being fully executed.

Article 16

Nothing in Articles 10, 11 and 14 shall be regarded as preventing the High Contracting Parties from imposing restrictions on the political activity of aliens.

Article 17

Nothing in this Convention may be interpreted as implying for any State group or person any right to engage in any activity or perform any act aimed at the destruction of any of the rights and freedoms set forth herein or at their limitation to a greater extent than is provided for in the Convention.

Article 18

The restrictions permitted under this Convention to the said rights and freedoms shall not be applied for any purpose other than those for which they have been prescribed.

SECTION II

Article 19

To ensure the observance of the engagements undertaken by the High Contracting Parties in the present Convention, there shall be set up:

(1) A European Commission of Human Rights hereinafter referred to as ''the Commission'';

(2) A European Court of Human Rights, hereinafter referred to as ''the Court''.

SECTION III

Article 20

The Commission shall consist of a number of members equal to that of the High Contracting Parties. No two members of the Commission may be nationals of the same State.

Article 21

1. The members of the Commission shall be elected by the Committee of Ministers by an absolute majority of votes, from a list of names drawn up by the Bureau of the Consultative Assembly; each group of the Representatives of the High Contracting Parties in the Consultative Assembly shall put forward three candidates, of whom two at least shall be its nationals.

2. As far as applicable, the same procedure shall be followed to complete the Commission in the event of other States subsequently becoming Parties to this Convention, and in filling casual vacancies.

Article 22

1. The members of the Commission shall be elected for a period of six years. They may be re-elected. However, of the members elected at the first election, the terms of seven members shall expire at the end of three years.

2. The members whose terms are to expire at the end of the initial period of three years shall be chosen by lot by the Secretary General of the Council of Europe immediately after the first election has been completed.

3. In order to ensure that, as far as possible, one half of the membership of the Commission shall be renewed every three years, the Committee of Ministers may decide, before proceeding to any subsequent election, that the term or terms of office of one or more members to be elected shall be for a period other than six years but not more than nine and not less than three years.

4. In cases where more than one term of office is involved and the Committee of Ministers applies the preceding paragraph, the allocation of the terms of office shall be effected by the drawing of lots by the Secretary General, immediately after the election.

5. A member of the Commission elected to replace a member whose term of office has not expired shall hold office for the remainder of his predecessor's term.

6. The members of the Commission shall hold office until replaced. After having been replaced, they shall continue to deal with such cases as they already have under consideration.

Article 23

The members of the Commission shall sit on the Commission in their individual capacity.

Article 24

Any High Contracting Party may refer to the Commission, through the Secretary General of the Council of Europe, any alleged breach of the provisions of the Convention by another High Contracting Party.

Article 25

1. The Commission may receive petitions addressed to the Secretary General of the Council of Europe from any person, non-governmental organisation or group of individuals

claiming to be the victim of a violation by one of the High Contracting Parties of the rights set forth in this Convention, provided that the High Contracting Party against which the complaint has been lodged has declared that it recognises the competence of the Commission to receive such petitions. Those of the High Contracting Parties who have made such a declaration undertake not to hinder in any way the effective exercise of this right.

2. Such declarations may be made for a specific period.

3. The declarations shall be deposited with the Secretary General of the Council of Europe who shall transmit copies thereof to the High Contracting parties and publish them.

4. The Commission shall only exercise the powers provided for in this Article when at least six High Contracting Parties are bound by declarations made in accordance with the preceding paragraphs.

Article 26

The Commission may only deal with the matter after all domestic remedies have been exhausted, according to the generally recognised rules of international law, and within a period of six months from the date on which the final decision was taken.

Article 27

1. The Commission shall not deal with any petition submitted under Article 25 which

(a) is anonymous, or

(b) is substantially the same as a matter which has already been examined by the Commission or has already been submitted to another procedure of international investigation or settlement and if it contains no relevant new information.

2. The Commission shall consider inadmissible any petition submitted under Article 25 which it considers incompatible with the provisions of the present Convention, manifestly ill-founded or an abuse of the right of petition.

3. The Commission shall reject any petition referred to it which it considers inadmissible under Article 26.

Article 28

In the event of the Commission accepting a petition referred to it:

(a) it shall, with a view to ascertaining the facts, undertake together with the representatives of the parties an examination of the petition and, if need be, an investigation, for the effective conduct of which the States concerned shall furnish all necessary facilities, after an exchange of views with the Commission;

(b) it shall place itself at the disposal of the parties concerned with a view to securing a friendly settlement of the matter on the basis of respect for Human Rights as defined in this Convention.

Article 29

After it has accepted a petition submitted under Article 25, the Commission may nevertheless decide unanimously to reject the petition if, in the course of its examination, it finds that the existence of one of the grounds for non-acceptance provided for in Article 27 has been established.

In such a case, the decision shall be communicated to the parties.

Article 30

If the Commission succeeds in effecting a friendly settlement in accordance with Article 28, it shall draw up a Report which shall be sent to the States concerned, to the Committee of Ministers and to the Secretary General of the Council of Europe for publication. This Report shall be confined to a brief statement of the facts and of the solution reached.

Article 31

1. If a solution is not reached, the Commission shall draw up a Report on the facts and state its opinion as to whether the

facts found disclose a breach by the State concerned of its obligations under the Convention. The opinions of all the members of the Commission on this point may be stated in the Report.

2. The Report shall be transmitted to the Committee of Ministers. It shall also be transmitted to the States concerned, who shall not be at liberty to publish it.

3. In transmitting the Report to the Committee of Ministers the Commission may make such proposals as it thinks fit.

Article 32

1. If the question is not referred to the Court in accordance with Article 48 of this Convention within a period of three months from the date of the transmission of the Report to the Committee of Ministers, the Committee of Ministers shall decide by a majority of two-thirds of the members entitled to sit on the Committee whether there has been a violation of the Convention.

2. In the affirmative case the Committee of Ministers shall prescribe a period during which the High Contracting Party concerned must take the measures required by the decision of the Committee of Ministers.

3. If the High Contracting Party concerned has not taken satisfactory measures within the prescribed period, the Committee of Ministers shall decide by the majority provided for in paragraph 1 above what effect shall be given to its original decision and shall publish the Report.

4. The High Contracting Parties undertake to regard as binding on them any decision which the Committee of Ministers may take in application of the preceding paragraphs.

Article 33

The Commission shall meet *in camera*.

Article 34

Subject to the provisions of Article 29, the Commission shall take its decisions by a majority of the Members present and voting.

Article 35

The Commission shall meet as the circumstances require. The meetings shall be convened by the Secretary General of the Council of Europe.

Article 36

The Commission shall draw up its own rules of procedure.

Article 37

The secretariat of the Commission shall be provided by the Secretary General of the Council of Europe.

SECTION IV

Article 38

The European Court of Human Rights shall consist of a number of judges equal to that of the Members of the Council of Europe. No two judges may be nationals of the same State.

Article 39

1. The members of the Court shall be elected by the Consultative Assembly by a majority of the votes cast from a list of persons nominated by the Members of the Council of Europe; each Member shall nominate three candidates, of whom two at least shall be its nationals.

2. As far as applicable, the same procedure shall be followed to complete the Court in the event of the admission of new Members of the Council of Europe, and in filling casual vacancies.

3. The candidates shall be of high moral character and must either posses the qualifications required for appointment to high judicial office or be jurisconsults of recognised competence.

Article 40

1. The members of the Court shall be elected for a period of nine years. They may be re-elected. However, of the mem-

bers elected at the first election the terms of four members shall expire at the end of three years, and the terms of four more members shall expire at the end of six years.

2. The members whose terms are to expire at the end of the initial periods of three and six years shall be chosen by lot by the Secretary General immediately after the first election has been completed.

3. In order to ensure that, as far as possible, one third of the membership of the Court shall be renewed every three years, the Consultative Assembly may decide, before proceeding to any subsequent election, that the term or terms of office of one or more members to be elected shall be for a period other than nine years but not more than twelve and not less than six years.

4. In cases where more than one term of office is involved and the Consultative Assembly applies the preceding paragraph, the allocation of the terms of office shall be effected by the drawing of lots by the Secretary General immediately after the election.

5. A member of the Court elected to replace a member whose term of office has not expired shall hold office for the remainder of his predecessor's term.

6. The members of the Court shall hold office until replaced. After having been replaced, they shall continue to deal with such cases as they already have under consideration.

Article 41

The Court shall elect its President and Vice-President for a period of three years. They may be re-elected.

Article 42

The members of the Court shall receive for each day of duty a compensation to be determined by the Committee of Ministers.

Article 43

For the consideration of each case brought before it the

Court shall consist of a Chamber composed of seven judges. There shall sit as an ex officio member of the Chamber the judge who is a national of any State party concerned, or, if there is none, a person of its choice who shall sit in the capacity of judge; the names of the other judges shall be chosen by lot by the President before the opening of the case.

Article 44

Only the High Contracting Parties and the Commission shall have the right to bring a case before the Court.

Article 45

The jurisdiction of the Court shall extend to all cases concerning the interpretation and application of the present Convention which the High Contracting Parties or the Commission shall refer to it in accordance with Article 48.

Article 46

1. Any of the High Contracting Parties may at any time declare that it recognises as compulsory *ipso facto* and without special agreement the jurisdiction of the Court in all matters concerning the interpretation and application of the present Convention.

2. The declarations referred to above may be made unconditionally or on condition of reciprocity on the part of several or certain other High Contracting Parties or for a specified period.

3. These declarations shall be deposited with the Secretary General of the Council of Europe who shall transmit copies thereof to the High Contracting Parties.

Article 47

The Court may only deal with a case after the Commission has acknowledged the failure of efforts for a friendly settlement and within the period of three months provided for in Article 32.

Article 48

The following may bring a case before the Court, provided

that the High Contracting Party concerned, if there is only one, or the High Contracting Parties concerned, if there is more than one, are subject to the compulsory jurisdiction of the Court or, failing that, with the consent of the High Contracting Party concerned, if there is only one, or of the High Contracting Parties concerned if there is more than one:

(a) the Commission;

(b) a High Contracting Party whose national is alleged to be a victim;

(c) a High Contracting Party which referred the case to the Commission:

(d) a High Contracting Party against which the complaint has been lodged.

Article 49

In the event of dispute as to whether the Court has jurisdiction, the matter shall be settled by decision of the Court.

Article 50

If the Court finds that a decision or a measure taken by a legal authority or any other authority of a High Contracting Party, is completely or partially in conflict with the obligations arising from the present Convention, and if the internal law of the said Party allows only partial reparation to be made for the consequences of this decision or measure, the decision of the Court shall, if necessary, afford just satisfaction to the injured party.

Article 51

1. Reasons shall be given for the judgment of the Court.

2. If the judgment does not represent in whole or in part the unanimous opinion of the judges, any judge shall be entitled to deliver a separate opinion.

Article 52

The judgment of the Court shall be final.

Article 53

The High Contracting Parties undertake to abide by the decision of the Court in any case to which they are parties.

Article 54

The judgment of the Court shall be transmitted to the Committee of Ministers which shall supervise its execution.

Article 55

The Court shall draw up its own rules and shall determine its own procedure.

Article 56

1. The first election of the members of the Court shall take place after the declarations by the High Contracting Parties mentioned in Article 46 have reached a total of eight.

2. No case can be brought before the Court before this election.

SECTION V

Article 57

On receipt of a request from the Secretary General of the Council of Europe any High Contracting Party shall furnish an explanation of the manner in which its internal law ensures the effective implementation of any of the provisions of this Convention.

Article 58

The expenses of the Commission and the Court shall be borne by the Council of Europe.

Article 59

The members of the Commission and of the Court shall be entitled, during the discharge of their functions, to the privileges and immunities provided for in Article 40 of the Statute of the Council of Europe and in the agreements made thereunder.

Article 60

Nothing in this Convention shall be construed as limiting or derogating from any of the human rights and fundamental freedoms which may be ensured under the laws of any High Contracting Party or under any other agreement to which it is a Party.

Article 61

Nothing in this Convention shall prejudice the powers conferred on the Committee of Ministers by the Statute of the Council of Europe.

Article 62

The High Contracting Parties agree that, except by special agreement, they will not avail themselves of treaties, conventions or declarations in force between them for the purpose of submitting, by way of petition, a dispute arising out of the interpretation or application of this Convention to a means of settlement other than those provided for in this Convention.

Article 63

1. Any State may at the time of its ratification or at any time thereafter declare by notification addressed to the Secretary General of the Council of Europe that the present Convention shall extend to all or any of the territories for whose international relations it is responsible.

2. The Convention shall extend to the territory or territories named in the notification as from the thirtieth day after the receipt of this notification by the Secretary General of the Council of Europe.

3. The provisions of this Convention shall be applied in such territories with due regard, however, to local requirements.

4. Any State which has made a declaration in accordance

with paragraph 1 of this Article may at any time thereafter declare on behalf of one or more of the territories to which the declaration relates that it accepts the competence of the Commission to receive petitions from individuals, non-governmental organisations or groups of individuals in accordance with Article 25 of the present Convention.

Article 64

1. Any State may, when signing this Convention or when depositing its instrument of ratification, make a reservation in respect of any particular provision of the Convention to the extent that any law then in force in its territory is not in conformity with the provision. Reservations of a general character shall not be permitted under this Article.

2. Any reservation made under this Article shall contain a brief statement of the law concerned.

Article 65

1. A High Contracting Party may denounce the present Convention only after the expiry of five years from the date on which it became a Party to it and after six months notice contained in a notification addressed to the Secretary General of the Council of Europe, who shall inform the other High Contracting Parties.

2. Such a denunciation shall not have the effect of releasing the High Contracting Party concerned from its obligations under this Convention in respect of any act which, being capable of constituting a violation of such obligations, may have been performed by it before the date at which the denunciation became effective.

3. Any High Contracting Party which shall cease to be a Member of the Council of Europe shall cease to be a Party to this Convention under the same conditions.

4. The Convention may be denounced in accordance with the provisions of the preceding paragraphs in respect of any territory to which it has been declared to extend under the terms of Article 63.

Article 66

1. This Convention shall be open to the signature of the Members of the Council of Europe. It shall be ratified. Ratifications shall be deposited with the Secretary General of the Council of Europe.

2. The present Convention shall come into force after the deposit of ten instruments of ratification.

3. As regards any signatory ratifying subsequently, the Convention shall come into force at the date of the deposit of its instrument of ratification.

4. The Secretary General of the Council of Europe shall notify all the Members of the Council of Europe of the entry into force of the Convention, the names of the High Contracting Parties who have ratified it, and the deposit of all instruments of ratification which may be effected subsequently.

DONE at Rome this 4th day of November 1950, in English and French, both texts being equally authentic, in a single copy which shall remain deposited in the archives of the Council of Europe. The Secretary General shall transmit certified copies to each of the signatories.

FIRST PROTOCOL TO THE CONVENTION

The Governments signatory hereto, being Members of the Council of Europe,

Being resolved to take steps to ensure the collective enforcement of certain rights and freedoms other than those already included in Section I of the Convention for the Protection of Human Rights and Fundamental Freedoms signed at Rome on 4th November, 1950 (hereinafter referred to as "the Convention").

Have agreed as follows:

Article 1

Every natural or legal person is entitled to the peaceful enjoyment of his possessions. No one shall be deprived of his possessions except in the public interest and subject to the conditions provided for by law and by the general principles of international law.

The preceding provisions shall not, however, in any way impair the right of a State to enforce such laws as it deems necessary to control the use of property in accordance with the general interest or to secure the payment of taxes or other contributions or penalties.

Article 2

No person shall be denied the right to education. In the exercise of any functions which it assumes in relation to education and to teaching, the State shall respect the right of parents to ensure such education and teaching in conformity with their own religious and philosophical convictions.

Article 3

The High Contracting Parties undertake to hold free elections at reasonable intervals by secret ballot, under conditions which will ensure the free expression of the opinion of the people in the choice of the legislature.

Article 4

Any High Contracting Party may at the time of signature or ratification or at any time thereafter communicate to the Secretary General of the Council of Europe a declaration stating the extent to which it undertakes that the provisions of the present Protocol shall apply to such of the territories for the international relations of which it is responsible as are named therein.

Any High Contracting Party which has communicated a declaration in virtue of the preceding paragraph may from time to time communicate a further declaration modifying the terms of any former declaration or terminating the application of the provisions of this Protocol in respect of any territory.

A declaration made in accordance with this Article shall be deemed to have been made in accordance with paragraph (1) of Article 63 of the Convention.

Article 5

As between the High Contracting Parties the provisions of Articles 1,2,3 and 4 of this Protocol shall be regarded as additional Articles to the Convention and all the provisions of the Convention shall apply accordingly.

Article 6

This Protocol shall be open for signature by the Members of the Council of Europe, who are the signatories of the Convention; it shall be ratified at the same time as or after the ratification of the Convention. It shall enter into force after the deposit of ten instruments of ratification. As regards any signatory ratifying subsequently, the Protocol shall enter into force at the date of the deposit of its instrument of ratification:

The instruments of ratification shall be deposited with the Secretary General of the Council of Europe, who will notify all Members of the names of those who have ratified.

Done at Paris on the 20th day of March 1952, in English and French, both texts being equally authentic, in a single copy which shall remain deposited in the archives of the Council of Europe. The Secretary General shall transmit certified copies to each of the signatory Governments.

Second Protocol

conferring upon the European Court of Human Rights
competence to give advisory opinions

The member States of the Council of Europe signatory hereto:

Having regard to the provisions of the Convention for the Protection of Human Rights and Fundamental Freedoms signed at Rome on 4th November 1950 (hereinafter referred to as "the Convention") and, in particular, Article 19 instituting, among other bodies, a European Court of Human Rights (hereinafter referred to as "the Court"):

Considering that it is expedient to confer upon the Court

competence to give advisory opinions subject to certain conditions.

Have agreed as follows:

Article 1

1. The Court may, at the request of the Committee of Ministers, give advisory opinions on legal questions concerning the interpretation of the Convention and the Protocols thereto.

2. Such opinions shall not deal with any question relating to the content or scope of the rights or freedoms defined in Section I of the Convention and in the Protocols thereto, or with any other question which the Commission, the Court or the Committee of Ministers might have to consider in consequence of any such proceedings as could be instituted in accordance with the Convention.

3. Decisions of the Committee of Ministers to request an advisory opinion of the Court shall require a two-thirds majority vote of the representatives entitled to sit on the Committee.

Article 2

The Court shall decide whether a request for an advisory opinion submitted by the Committee of Ministers is within its consultative competence as defined in Article 1 of this Protocol.

Article 3

1. For the consideration of requests for an advisory opinion, the Court shall sit in plenary session.

2. Reasons shall be given for advisory opinions of the Court.

3. If the advisory opinion does not represent in whole or in part the unanimous opinion of the judges, any judge shall be entitled to deliver a separate opinion.

4. Advisory opinions of the Court shall be communicated to the Committee of Ministers.

Article 4

The powers of the Court under Article 55 of the Convention shall extend to the drawing up of such rules and the determination of such procedure as the Court may think necessary for the purposes of this Protocol.

Article 5

1. This Protocol shall be open to signature by member States of the Council of Europe, signatories to the Convention, who may become Parties to it by:

(a) signature without reservation in respect of ratification or acceptance:

(b) signature with reservation in respect of ratification or acceptance, followed by ratification or acceptance.

Instruments of ratification or acceptance shall be deposited with the Secretary General of the Council of Europe.

2. This Protocol shall enter into force as soon as all States Parties to the Convention shall have become Parties to the Protocol, in accordance with the provisions of paragraph 1 of this Article.

3. From the date of the entry into force of this Protocol, Articles 1 to 4 shall be considered an integral part of the Convention.

4. The Secretary General of the Council of Europe shall notify the member States of the Council of:

(a) any signature without reservation in respect of ratification or acceptance;

(b) any signature with reservation in respect of ratification or acceptance;

(c) the deposit of any instrument of ratification or acceptance;

(d) the date of entry into force of this Protocol in accordance with paragraph 2 of this Article.

In witness whereof, the undersigned, being duly authorised thereto, have signed this Protocol.

Done at Strasbourg, this 6th day of May 1963, in English and in French, both texts being equally authoritative, in a single copy which shall remain deposited in the archives of the Council of Europe. The Secretary General shall transmit certified copies to each of the signatory States.

Fourth Protocol

securing certain rights and freedoms
other than those already included in the Convention
and in the first Protocol thereto

The Governments signatory hereto, being Members of the Council of Europe,

Being resolved to take steps to ensure the collective enforcement of certain rights and freedoms other than those already included in Section I of the Convention for the Protection of Human Rights and Fundamental Freedoms signed at Rome on 4th November 1950 (hereinafter referred to as "the Convention") and in Articles 1 to 3 of the First Protocol to the Convention, signed at Paris on 20th March 1952,

Have agreed as follows:

Article 1

No one shall be deprived of his liberty merely on the ground of inability to fulfill a contractual obligation.

Article 2

1. Everyone lawfully within the territory of a State shall, within that territory, have the right to liberty of movement and freedom to choose his residence.

2. Everyone shall be free to leave any country, including his own.

3. No restrictions shall be placed on the exercise of these rights other than such as are in accordance with law and are

necessary in a democratic society in the interests of national security or public safety, for the maintenance of *ordre public,* for the prevention of crime, for the protection of health or morals, or for the protection of the rights and freedoms of others.

4. The rights set forth in paragraph 1 may also be subject, in particular areas, to restrictions imposed in accordance with law and justified by the public interest in democratic society.

Article 3

1. No one shall be expelled, by means either of an individual or of a collective measure, from the territory of the State of which he is a national.

2. No one shall be deprived of the right to enter the territory of the State of which he is a national.

Article 4

Collective expulsion of aliens is prohibited.

Article 5

1. Any High Contracting Pary may, at the time of signature or ratification of this Protocol, or at any time thereafter, communicate to the Secretary General of the Council of Europe a declaration stating the extent to which it undertakes that the provisions of this Protocol shall apply to such of the territories for the international relations of which it is responsible as are named therein.

2. Any High Contracting Party which has communicated a declaration in virtue of the preceding paragraph may, from time to time, communicate a further declaration modifying the terms of any former declaration or terminating the application of the provisions of this Protocol in respect of any territory.

3. A declaration made in accordance with this Article shall be deemed to have been made in accordance with paragraph 1 of Article 63 of the Convention.

4. The territory of any State to which this protocol applies

by virtue of ratification or acceptance by that State, and each territory to which this Protocol is applied by virtue of a declaration by that State under this Article, shall be treated as separate territories for the purpose of the references in Articles 2 and 3 to the territory of a State.

Article 6

1. As between the High Contracting Parties the provisions of Articles 1 to 5 of this Protocol shall be regarded as additional Articles to the Convention, and all the provisions of the Convention shall apply accordingly.

2. Nevertheless, the right of individual recourse recognised by a declaration made under Article 25 of the Convention, or the acceptance of the compulsory jurisdiction of the Court by a declaration made under Article 46 of the Convention, shall not be effective in relation to this Protocol unless the High Contracting Party concerned has made a statement recognising such right, or accepting such jurisdiction, in respect of all or any of Articles 1 to 4 of the Protocol.

Article 7

1. This Protocol shall be open for signature by the Members of the Council of Europe who are the signatories of the Convention; it shall be ratified at the same time as or after the ratification of the Convention. It shall enter into force after the deposit of five instruments of ratification. As regards any signatory ratifying subsequently, the Protocol shall enter into force at the date of the deposit of its instrument of ratification.

2. The instruments of ratification shall be deposited with the Secretary General of the Council of Europe, who will notify all Members of the names of those who have ratified.

In witness whereof, the undersigned, being duly authorised thereto, have signed this Protocol.

Done at Strasbourg, this 16th day of September 1963, in English and in French, both texts being equally authoritative, in a single copy which shall remain deposited in the archives of the Council of Europe. The Secretary General shall transmit certified copies to each of the signatory States.

Chart showing the state of Ratifications
and optional Declarations relating to the European
Convention on Human Rights and its Protocols[1]

Member States of the Council of Europe Entry into force	Convention[2] 3 9 53	Declarations		Protocol n°1 18 5 54	Protocol n°2 21 9 70	Protocol n°4 2 5 68
		Individual Petitions (Art. 25)	Jurisdiction of the Court			
Austria						
Belgium						
Cyprus		▨	▨			▨
Denmark						
France		▨			▨	
Federal Republic of Germany						
Greece		▨	▨			▨
Iceland						
Ireland						
Italy						
Luxembourg						
Malta		▨	▨			▨
Netherlands						
Norway						
Portugal		▨	▨			▨
Spain		▨	▨	▨	▨	▨
Sweden						
Switzerland						▨
Turkey		▨	▨			▨
United Kingdom						

1. As at 1 January 1978
2. As amended by Protocols n°3 and n°5

☐ ratified or declaration made   ▨ not signed or no declaration made

INDEXES

AUTHOR INDEX

SUBJECT INDEX